Securing Rig
for Victims

A Process Evaluation of the National Crime Victim Law Institute's Victims' Rights Clinics

Robert C. Davis, James M. Anderson,
Julie Whitman, Susan Howley

Sponsored by the National Institute of Justice

RAND

Safety and Justice

A RAND INFRASTRUCTURE, SAFETY, AND ENVIRONMENT PROGRAM

The research described in this report was sponsored by the National Institute of Justice and was conducted under the auspices of the Safety and Justice Program of RAND Infrastructure, Safety, and Environment (ISE).

Library of Congress Cataloging-in-Publication Data

Securing rights for victims : a process evaluation of the National Crime Victim Law Institute's victims' rights clinics / Robert C. Davis ... [et al.].
p. cm.
Includes bibliographical references.
ISBN 978-0-8330-4890-5 (pbk. : alk. paper)
1. Victims of crimes—Legal status, laws, etc.—United States.
I. Davis, Robert C. (Robert Carl)

KF9763.S43 2009
344.7303'288—dc22

2009042236

Published 2009 by the RAND Corporation
1776 Main Street, P.O. Box 2138, Santa Monica, CA 90407-2138
1200 South Hayes Street, Arlington, VA 22202-5050
4570 Fifth Avenue, Suite 600, Pittsburgh, PA 15213-2665
RAND URL: http://www.rand.org/
To order RAND documents or to obtain additional information, contact
Distribution Services: Telephone: (310) 451-7002;
Fax: (310) 451-6915; Email: order@rand.org

Preface

This is the final process-evaluation report of the National Crime Victim Law Institute's victims' rights clinics. The evaluation was funded by the National Institute of Justice (NIJ). The clinics were designed to increase awareness of victims' rights among criminal-justice professionals and to respond to violations of rights through legal advocacy. The monograph is based on case studies of the individual state clinics. The body of the monograph synthesizes commonalities of experiences among the individual clinics, as well as differences in their approaches and environments. Three appendixes, available online (see Davis et al., 2009), supplement the text here: Appendix A provides the site reports; Appendix B lists statutory and case law changes in clinic states; and Appendix C gives the interview topics. The monograph and its appendixes are intended for an audience of researchers and criminal-justice practitioners interested in victims' rights. The process evaluation will be followed up by an impact evaluation in the upcoming 18 months.

Readers of this monograph may be interested in other RAND reports on the justice system, such as the following:

- *Oregon's Measure 11 Sentencing Reform: Implementation and System Impact* (Merritt, Fain, and Turner, 2004)
- *Just Cause or Just Because? Prosecution and Plea-Bargaining Resulting in Prison Sentences on Low-Level Drug Charges in California and Arizona* (Riley et al., 2005)
- *Race and the Decision to Seek the Death Penalty in Federal Cases* (Klein, Berk, and Hickman, 2006).

The RAND Safety and Justice Program

This research was conducted under the auspices of the Safety and Justice Program within RAND Infrastructure, Safety, and Environment (ISE). The mission of RAND ISE is to improve the development, operation, use, and protection of society's essential physical assets and natural resources and to enhance the related social assets of safety and security of individuals in transit and in their workplaces and communities. Safety and Justice Program research addresses occupational safety, transportation safety, food safety, and public safety—including violence, policing, corrections, substance abuse, and public integrity.

Questions or comments about this monograph should be sent to the project leader, Rob Davis (Rob_Davis@rand.org). Information about the Safety and Justice Program is available online (http://www.rand.org/ise/safety). Inquiries about research projects should be sent to the following address:

Greg Ridgeway, Director
Safety and Justice Program, ISE
RAND Corporation
1776 Main Street
P.O. Box 2138
Santa Monica, CA 90407-2138
310-393-0411, x7734
Greg_Ridgeway@rand.org

Contents

Figures

Tables

Summary

This monograph describes a process evaluation conducted by the RAND Corporation and National Center for Victims of Crime of the National Crime Victim Law Institute (NCVLI) state and federal victims' rights clinics. The clinics were conceived as a response to the fact that, in spite of burgeoning victims' rights legislation in all states, many victims still are not receiving the rights to which they are entitled under law. The NCVLI clinics were intended to promote awareness, education, and enforcement of crime victims' rights in the criminal-justice system.

In establishing the victims' rights clinics, NCVLI sought to change the legal culture with respect to observance of victims' rights. The vehicle for doing this was providing direct representation to individual victims in criminal court. By giving victims attorneys, NCVLI hoped that it could increase the observance of rights in those particular cases. But it also hoped that the presence of victims' attorneys in some cases and trainings held for court officials would result in an increased attention to victims' rights by prosecutors, judges, and police officers in all cases—not just in the cases in which victims were represented by attorneys.

Moreover, initiating strategic litigation at the appellate level was designed to expand judicial recognition of victims' rights in state and federal court. This could happen through published, or even unpublished, appellate-court opinions (case law) or through changes to court rules. In NCVLI's view, even losing cases at the appellate level could result in long-term gain; cases that are lost can clarify the law and show what victims' rights statutes actually mean. The new clarity may impel legislators to enact new and broader statutes.

The NCVLI clinics work to promote observance of victims' rights by representing victims in individual cases and by working to change the legal culture through example, training, and appellate decisions and court rules that acknowledge victims' rights. When they become aware of a potential rights violation, the first step may be to place a call to a criminal-justice official to see whether the condition can be easily remedied. For example, they may try to convince police to file a case with the court or to convince a prosecutor to advance a trial date. Or they may ask a prosecutor to oppose a defense motion to order a victim to release medical records. Clinic attorneys also file motions in trial courts on behalf of their clients. In some states, clinic attorneys have filed motions to amend a plea to include restitution or other conditions based on statutory rights. Other attorneys have filed writs with appeals courts to get victims admitted into the courtroom after they were denied the right to be present by a trial court judge. Finally, clinic attorneys work at the appellate level to seek published rulings that clarify or expand the scope of victim rights on critical issues, such as victim standing and privacy.

While clinics share these common interests and activities, they differ in how they are structured and how they operate. Differences along these dimensions have potential implications for the number and geographic diversity of cases that clinics handle, sources of client referrals, types of cases handled, and funding sustainability.

Evaluation Objectives

NIJ's evaluation plan proposed a two-part effort: a process evaluation that would be descriptive in nature, followed by an impact evaluation that would attempt to determine measurable benefits of the clinics.

For the process evaluation, we undertook an initial phase of work that developed case studies of NCVLI and the eight clinics.[1] The case studies of NCVLI and each of the eight clinics, presented in this monograph, examine the implementation process, the environments in which the clinics operate, problems encountered, and solutions. This monograph synthesizes commonalities of experiences among the eight clinics as well as differences in their approaches and environments. During the course of the process evaluation, we also constructed a logic model to describe the goals and measurable outcomes of the clinic's work, which was vetted with NCVLI. In the second phase of work, we will conduct theory-based evaluations of the effects that the clinics have had on enforcement of victims' rights in the criminal-justice system in the states and localities where they are based. This phase of work will be based on the clinic logic model refined during the earlier phase of work. The impact evaluation will assess the impact of the clinics on the individual, system, and community levels.

The process evaluation addresses a number of NIJ and Office of Victims of Crime (OVC) interests. First, it assesses implementation problems faced by the clinics: How were they accepted by the state criminal-justice community? How did they publicize their existence? From what sources did they get case referrals, and did the referral sources change over time? Second, an examination of ways in which the clinics have been able to leverage federal resources, particularly through the use of law students and pro bono attorneys: How successful have efforts been to recruit low-cost or free sources of labor? Is training for students or pro bono attorneys on victims' rights issues useful when they go on to other endeavors? Third, an evaluation of how successful clinics have been in changing the legal landscape: In what kinds of appellate decisions have they been involved as a party or in an amicus curiae ("friend of the court") capacity, and what is the significance of the cases? Have appellate losses led to changes in victims'

---

[1] The original number was nine clinics, counting Arizona's state and federal work as two separate clinics. However, the state and federal sides of Arizona's Crime Victim Legal Assistance Project have since merged into a single clinic; hence, this monograph deals with eight clinics.

rights statutes? Have there been changes to court rules that promote victims' rights? A list of topics covered in the process evaluation is contained in Table S.1.

Evaluation Methods

To gain information on these topics to construct the series of case studies, we carried out site visits to each of the clinics. During the multi-day visits, our principal source of information was interviews with the clinic director and staff. Clinic directors and their staff were all generous with their time and, we believe, forthcoming about their experiences and problems.

Each of the site visits included a focus group with victims who were past or present clients of the clinic. We requested that each clinic director attempt to recruit six to eight of the clinic's clients to participate in a 90-minute focus group. All were able to gather a group of victims who provided a client perspective on the clinics and helped us further refine questions and measures for the subsequent impact study. Illustrative focus-group topics included the following:

- How did they learn about the clinic?
- What types of services were provided by clinic staff?
- How did the services they received help them?
- Were they satisfied with the people who provided the services?
- What suggestions do they have for improving the criminal-justice process?

After each site visit, clinic staff abstracted information from their client files on the number of victims represented, types of cases and victims' rights issues in which the clinics were involved, county and court in which cases originated, clinic actions on behalf of victims and the results of those actions, and demographics of victims represented.

We also developed with each clinic director a list of positional informants—people in the criminal-justice community who were knowledgeable about the clinic's work. We requested that the list

Table S.1
Process-Evaluation Issues

Issue Area	Issue
Information about clinic activities	Major clinic activities and approximate proportion of staff time devoted to each Changes over time in clinic goals and activities No. of individual clients represented, no. of motions filed, no. of court appearances on behalf of clients, no. of trainings by clinic staff
Criminal-justice context	Geographic dispersion of courts in which clinic staff have represented clients Extent to which victims' rights statutes facilitate or hinder the work of the clinic Jurisdiction in which the clinic has done the most work (target jurisdiction) Receptivity of judges, prosecutors to victims' rights and work of the clinic Principal victim-service organizations; nature of cooperation with clinic
Pro bono staff	With how many pro bono attorneys has the clinic worked? How successful have these arrangements been?
Recruiting and screening mechanism for selecting clients	Eligibility criteria for representing victims (e.g., types of cases, types of issues) Sources through which clients are referred and any changes over time No. of cases identified or referrals determined to be eligible for clinic services; no. accepted No. of cases determined to be eligible that were not accepted for assistance; reasons for not taking cases Outreach mechanisms clinic staff use to identify and reach victims in need of assistance; any efforts made to reach underserved populations
Information for impact study	What do clinic staff believe are the best ways to assess the impact of their clinic? What data do they have to evaluate these program effects? How do they define success? Ways in which the clinic has changed the climate for victims' rights in state Any unintended consequences (positive or negative) of the clinic Would they be willing to participate in an impact study?
Suggestions to improve clinic operations	Obstacles faced in meeting clinic goals; steps taken to overcome those obstacles Suggestions to improve the effectiveness of the local clinic or effectiveness of NCLVI program generally

include both individuals supportive of the clinic's work and those who had been critics. Interviewing these individuals—judges, prosecutors, victims' advocates, and defense attorneys—was an important way to corroborate or challenge what we learned from the clinic staff (who, understandably, want to portray their program in the best light). The interviews with positional informants asked about respondents' opinions on the need for the clinics, on the work that the clinics are doing, and on the extent to which criminal-justice officials support victims' rights.

Research-project attorneys prepared a compendium of victims' rights legislation in the states of each clinic visited. They also summarized any appellate cases and published opinions about victims' rights.

For each site visited, we prepared a report describing the operations of the clinic and what we learned from all components of the site visit. The site reports described the legal context within which the clinics work, clinic operations, obstacles encountered and responses to those obstacles, and measures that would best assess clinic impact.

Finally, we conducted two visits to NCVLI offices in Portland, once at the start of the process evaluation and another after the clinic site visits had been completed. The interviews with NCVLI's director gathered information about the motivation and history of the clinic program and goals for the program. We also used the visits to gain feedback on our impressions and conclusions from the site visits.

Summary of Key Findings

There Is Great Diversity in the Ways in Which Clinics Have Been Structured

Clinics ranged in their organizational aegis from being housed within victim-service programs to being located within a law school to being one component within a full-service law firm. Each of these arrangements has implications for how the clinics function. Clinics with close connections with law schools gain stature from the affiliation, have access to free student labor, and have the potential to train students in victims' rights issues that they will carry with them into subsequent jobs as prosecutors, public defenders, guardians ad litem, or advocates for victims in civil cases. Clinics located within statewide victim-service providers enjoy reduced staff and space costs, enjoy the stature of the parent organization, benefit from extensive referral networks, and can work cooperatively with staff of the parent agency engaged in lobbying efforts. One clinic is affiliated with a private law firm, an arrangement that may offer a unique path to institutionalization through time and proceeds donated by the firm's attorneys to victims' rights work.

Although There Are Problems with the Use of Pro Bono Attorneys, They Hold Potential for Expanding the Volume of Cases That Clinics Handle and Their Geographic Coverage

Every clinic has made an effort to train pro bono attorneys and refer cases to them. The experience has not always been positive. Some clinic directors argued that pro bono attorneys seldom have the knowledge, commitment, or availability to be of significant help. However, there are obvious benefits to using pro bono help in a limited way to leverage the relatively small budgets on which clinics operate. The plans of some clinics to sponsor courses to train private attorneys who are seriously interested in victims' rights work should remove two of the objections to the use of pro bono attorneys: Taking a course will help ensure that volunteers are both interested and satisfactorily trained in victims' rights law.

While Their Primary Focus Has Always Been on Addressing Violations of Clients' Legal Rights, Most of the Clinics Have Developed a Focus That Includes Addressing All of Victims' Crime-Related Needs, Either Directly or Through Referrals to Other Service Providers

The fact that most clinics have concerned themselves with the totality of client needs—not just the potential value of cases in litigating rights issues—highlights the way in which the clinics' and NCVLI's approaches complement one another. Clinic attorneys appropriately act as client advocates for many crime-related needs. NCVLI, meanwhile, maintains its focus on changing the legal landscape and keeping an eye out for the cases that are likely to push its reform agenda significantly ahead.

Clinics Differ Substantially in Their Approaches and Methods of Operating

The number of cases opened annually differs substantially among the clinics, with the most prolific clinic handling a caseload eight times larger than the least prolific clinic. The cases of most clinics are concentrated in one or two counties, but one clinic demonstrated wide dispersion of cases across the state. Referral sources vary significantly, with some clinics receiving most referrals from prosecutors, others from victims' advocates, and still others from their Web sites or word of mouth. Clinics specialize in different types of cases—some in sexual assault, others in homicide or child abuse. Clinics also differ in their approach to representing clients, with some more inclined to use litigation as a first option and others more likely to try letters or phones calls first before resorting to litigation.

Standing Has Been the Threshold Issue That Clinics Have Had to Confront at the Trial-Court Level

Clinics have dealt with a range of victims' rights issues in trial courts, including the right to be present, right to be consulted about plea offers, right to make an impact statement, right to be notified of changes in defendants' detention status, right to restitution, and right to privacy. However, the principal issue has been victim standing before the court. In some states, standing has been acknowledged, at least in limited ways. In other states, clinics have made or are making steps toward such recognition or have been successful in representing victims without the issue being directly confronted. In one state, the ability of clinics to represent victims is currently in serious question.

Some Clinics Have Won Significant Gains at the Appellate and Federal Levels

The Maryland clinic has had three appellate cases related to victim standing that ultimately resulted in a newly expanded court rule giving victims the right to participate in a criminal appeal in the same manner as a party regarding issues that directly and substantially affect the victim's rights. The New Mexico clinic had one successful appellate case in 2006 on victim standing, and, although it resulted only in an unpublished opinion, the clinic has been successful in citing it as persuasive authority in other cases. Other clinics have been involved in appellate cases seeking relief for victims not properly notified of plea agreements, limits on defense efforts to subpoena victims' counseling records, and latitude to make specific sentencing recommendations in victims' impact statements. The Arizona clinic won a federal decision that affirmed that victims have "an indefeasible right to speak, similar to that of the defendant."

Conclusions

From the information we gathered during the course of the process evaluation, we believe that the state clinics are on the road to fulfilling the intentions of their architects and funders. All of the clinics have pushed the envelope of victims' rights in their state courts. Some have won significant victories in gaining standing for victims and expanding the definition of particular rights. Others are enjoined in the battle. But all have raised awareness of victims' rights with prosecutors, judges, defense attorneys, and police officials.

How far the clinics have managed to alter the legal culture remains to be determined through the second, or impact, phase of this evaluation. Two significant parts of that effort will be to (a) determine how court officials' opinions and observance of victims' rights have changed and (b) assess the extent to which basic victims' rights, such as being informed of rights or receiving restitution, have increased since the clinics opened. We plan to assess the former issue through systematic surveys with judges, prosecutors, victims' advocates, and defense attorneys who deal with felony cases and the latter issue through examination of case files before and after the clinics opened their doors.

One of the good things about how NCVLI has gone about setting up the state clinic program is that it has funded different clinic models, as defined by where the clinics are housed, the kinds of cases in which they tend to specialize, whether they are issue-focused or client-focused, whether they use litigation as a first or last resort, and how much use they make of pro bono attorneys or student help. This diversity creates the ability to compare the kinds of outcomes achieved by different models, in terms of the numbers and types of clients served, in terms of getting favorable published opinions or changes to court rules, and in terms of changing observance of victims' rights by court officials. It may prove that different clinic models are appropriate for certain things and other models appropriate for other things. For example, it may be that a successful pro bono program is associated with a greater number of clients served, while a focus on litigation is associated with successes in obtaining favorable published opinions on victims' rights.

One thing that the process evaluation has made clear is that clinics that build on the networks and reputations of experienced clinic directors and boards have an easier time of it than clinics that have to start from scratch. Clinics with directors and boards that are well connected gain more referrals and have more success getting prosecutors and judges to accede to their desired outcomes, even without having to litigate. A good part of their success may also result from trust that the directors have built up with local officials in their years of victims' rights work. It will be instructive to see whether the clinics starting from scratch are able to make up ground over time and develop the same kinds of respect and relationships that the Maryland, New Jersey, and Arizona clinics enjoy as a result of their directors' contacts or the Utah clinic enjoys as a result of contacts of board members.

The vision of NCVLI is being implemented by the clinics. It remains for further evaluation work to determine the extent to which the clinics have succeeded in changing the legal culture regarding victims' rights and encouraged greater observance of victims' rights in cases in which victims are unrepresented by counsel as well as those in which they are.

The monograph contains two sizable appendixes, available online (see Davis et al., 2009). Appendix A contains the individual site reports for each of the clinics visited. The individual site reports provide more detail from each site on issues discussed in the body of the monograph. Appendix B presents a detailed description of victims' rights legislation and case law in the eight NCVLI clinic states, which is summarized in Chapter Four. A third appendix, Appendix C, details the interview topics.

Abbreviations

AVCV	Arizona Voice for Crime Victims
CLE	continuing legal education
COVA	Colorado Organization for Victim Assistance
CVRA	Crime Victims' Rights Act
DOJ	U.S. Department of Justice
DWI	driving while intoxicated
IRB	Institutional Review Board
MCVRC	Maryland Crime Victims' Resource Center
NAACP	National Association for the Advancement of Colored People
NAVRA	National Alliance of Victims' Rights Attorneys
NCVLI	National Crime Victim Law Institute
NIJ	National Institute of Justice
OVC	Office for Victims of Crime
SCVAN	South Carolina Victim Assistance Network
TA	technical assistance
VOCA	Victims of Crime Act

CHAPTER ONE

Introduction

This monograph describes a process evaluation conducted by the RAND Corporation and National Center for Victims of Crime of the National Crime Victim Law Institute (NCVLI) state and federal victims' rights clinics. The clinics were conceived as a response to the fact that, in spite of burgeoning victims' rights legislation in all states, many victims still are not receiving the rights to which they are entitled under law. The NCVLI clinics were intended to promote awareness, education, and enforcement of crime victims' rights in the criminal-justice system.

The National Institute of Justice's (NIJ's) evaluation plan proposed a two-part effort: a process evaluation that would be descriptive in nature, followed by an impact evaluation that would attempt to determine measurable benefits of the clinics. We interpreted this to mean an initial phase of work that would feature case studies of NCVLI and the eight clinics.[1] The case studies of NCVLI and each of the eight clinics, presented in this monograph, examine the implementation process, the environments in which the clinics operate, problems encountered, and solutions. This monograph synthesizes commonalities of experiences among the eight clinics, as well as differences in their approaches and environments. During the course of the process evaluation, we also constructed a logic model to describe the goals

[1] The original number was nine clinics, counting Arizona's state and federal work as two separate clinics. However, the state and federal sides of Arizona's Crime Victims' Legal Assistance Project have since merged into a single clinic; hence, this monograph deals with eight clinics.

and measurable outcomes of the clinic's work, which was vetted with NCVLI. In the second phase of work, we will conduct theory-based evaluations of the effects that the clinics have had on enforcement of victims' rights in the criminal-justice system in the states and localities where they are based. This phase of work will be based on the clinic logic model refined during the earlier phase of work. The impact evaluation will assess the impact of the clinics on the individual, system, and community levels.

Topics Addressed in the Process Evaluation

The process evaluation addresses a number of NIJ Office for Victims of Crime (OVC) interests:

- an assessment of implementation problems faced by the clinics: How were they accepted by the state criminal-justice community? How did they publicize their existence? From what sources did they get case referrals, and did the referral sources change over time?
- an examination of ways in which the clinics have been able to leverage federal resources, particularly through the use of law students and pro bono attorneys: How successful have efforts been to recruit low-cost or free sources of labor? Is training that students or pro bono attorneys receive on victims' rights issues useful when they go on to other endeavors?
- an evaluation of how successful clinics have been in changing the legal landscape: What kinds of appellate decisions have they been involved in as a party or in an amicus curiae (friend of the court) capacity, and what is the significance of the cases? Have appellate losses led to changes in victims' rights statutes? Have there been changes to court rules that promote enforcement of victims' rights? A list of topics covered in the process evaluation is contained in Table 1.1.

Table 1.1
Process-Evaluation Issues

Issue Area	Issue
Information about clinic activities	Major clinic activities and approximate proportion of staff time devoted to each Changes over time in clinic goals and activities No. of individual clients represented, no. of motions filed, no. of court appearances on behalf of clients, no. of trainings by clinic staff
Criminal-justice context	Geographic dispersion of courts in which clinic staff have represented clients Extent to which victims' rights statutes facilitate or hinder the work of the clinic Jurisdiction in which the clinic has done the most work (target jurisdiction) Receptivity of judges, prosecutors to victims' rights and work of the clinic Principal victim-service organizations; nature of cooperation with clinic
Pro bono staff	With how many pro bono attorneys has the clinic worked? How successful have these arrangements been?
Recruiting and screening mechanism for selecting clients	Eligibility criteria for representing victims (e.g., types of cases, types of issues) Sources through which clients are referred and any changes over time No. of cases identified or referrals determined to be eligible for clinic services; no. accepted No. of cases determined to be eligible that were not accepted for assistance; reasons for not taking cases Outreach mechanisms clinic staff use to identify and reach victims in need of assistance; any efforts made to reach underserved populations
Information for impact study	What do clinic staff believe are the best ways to assess the impact of their clinic? What data do they have to evaluate these program effects? How do they define success? Ways in which the clinic has changed the climate for victims' rights in state Any unintended consequences (positive or negative) of the clinic Would they be willing to participate in an impact study?
Suggestions to improve clinic operations	Obstacles faced in meeting clinic goals; steps taken to overcome those obstacles Suggestions to improve the effectiveness of the local clinic or effectiveness of NCLVI program generally

Evaluation Methods

Much of the information for the process evaluation came from interviews conducted with clinic staff, criminal-justice officials familiar with the work of the clinics, and clients of the clinics. Initially, we sought and received approval for interview procedures, informed-consent statements, and data-safeguarding procedures from RAND's Institutional Review Board (IRB). In all interviews conducted, one project staff person had principal responsibility for asking questions from a list of topics and another staff person took written notes.

To gain information on the topics listed in Table 1.1 to construct the series of case studies, we carried out site visits to each of the clinics. During the multiday visits, our principal source of information came from interviews with the clinic director and staff. Clinic directors and their staff were all generous with their time and, we believe, forthcoming about their experiences and problems. A list of topics covered in the interviews is contained in Appendix C (see Davis et al., 2009).

Each of the site visits entailed one or more focus groups with victims who were past or present clients of the clinic. We requested that each clinic director attempt to recruit six to eight of that clinic's clients to participate in a 90-minute focus group. All were able to gather a group of victims who provided a client perspective on the clinics and helped us further refine questions and measures for the subsequent impact study. Illustrative focus-group topics included the following:

- How did they learn about the clinic?
- What types of services were provided by clinic staff?
- How did the services they received help them?
- Were they satisfied with the people who provided the services?
- What suggestions do they have for improving the criminal-justice process?

Victims received a stipend of $25 to cover the cost of travel to the 1.5-hour meeting. (Some participants traveled as long as two hours to participate.) We did not record names of the participants, and notes of the meetings do not contain identifiers.

It was our aim to collect, from each clinic, information on the number of victims represented, types of cases and victims' rights issues in which the clinics were involved, county and court in which cases originated, clinic actions on behalf of victims and the results of those actions, and demographics of victims represented. Because of confidentiality concerns, it was not possible for the research staff to abstract information from the files. Instead, staff at each clinic agreed to gather the information for us according to our instructions. This raises some concerns about the consistency of how information was categorized, especially information on the types of rights issues in clinic cases. If a victim failed to be consulted about a potential plea agreement, for example, one clinic may have coded the rights issue as failure to be consulted about a plea agreement, while another may have coded it as a violation of the victim's right to be notified and present.

Moreover, it turned out that clinics collected little or no demographic information on clients. We believed (and still do) that one of the important questions about the clinics is whom they are representing. There is reason to suspect that the relatively few victims who become clients (of the large number who probably have their rights violated in one way or another) tend to be especially vocal and aggressive—and probably better educated and relatively well off. One of the questions that we would have liked to address in the process evaluation is what the demographic profile of clients looks like. Although information was not available during the process-evaluation period to answer this question, NCVLI did instruct the clinics to begin to gather basic demographic information on new cases in the fall of 2008. Within a few months, there should be enough new cases in each site to begin to create profiles of each clinic's clientele.

While we were on site, we developed with each clinic director a list of positional informants—people in the criminal-justice community who were knowledgeable about the clinic's work. We requested that the list include both individuals supportive of the clinic's work and those who had been critics. Interviewing these individuals—judges, prosecutors, victims' advocates, and defense attorneys—was an important way to corroborate or challenge what we learned from the clinic staff (who understandably want to portray their program in the best light). We aimed to interview two individuals within each of the aforementioned four groups of criminal-justice professionals, and, in most instances, we met that goal. The 15- to 20-minute interviews with positional informants asked about respondents' opinions on the need for the clinics, on the work that the clinics are doing, and on the extent to which criminal-justice officials support victims' rights. Because the clinic directors handpicked the individuals interviewed, we cannot know whether the samples were representative of professional opinions of the clinics. We do know, however, that we did encounter in the interviews statements that were critical of aspects of the clinics' work. Refer to Appendix C (see Davis et al., 2009) for topics covered in interviews with positional informants.

Research-project attorneys prepared a compendium of victims' rights legislation in the state of each clinic visited. They also summarized any appellate cases and published opinions about victims' rights. We attempted to ascertain from the clinics in which of these legislative and case-law developments the clinic staff had been involved.

For each site visited, we prepared a report describing the operations of the clinic and what we learned from all components of the site visit. The site reports described the legal context within which the clinics work, clinic operations, obstacles encountered and responses to those obstacles, and measures that would best assess clinic impact.

Finally, we conducted two visits to NCVLI offices in Portland, Oregon—one at the start of the process evaluation and another after the clinic site visits had been completed. The interviews with NCVLI's director gathered information about the motivation and history of the clinic program and goals for the program. We also used the visits to gain feedback on our impressions and conclusions from the site visits.

Layout of the Monograph

The body of this monograph summarizes what we have learned during the course of the process evaluation. Following this introduction, Chapter Two discusses the development of victims' rights in the United States. Chapter Three describes NCVLI and the goals of the clinics.

Chapter Four summarizes changes to the legal landscape for victims' rights in the states where the clinics are located, both through appellate cases and through changes in victims' rights statutes, some of which clinic cases have instigated. Chapter Five describes clinic operations—the types of business models adopted by the clinics, their experience with pro bono attorneys and student help, and their approach to serving their clientele. Chapter Six presents data gathered from clinic case files on referral sources, caseload size and composition, types of rights issues dealt with by the clinics, and geographic diversity of the clinics' case loads. Chapters Seven and Eight deal with clinic work at the trial court and appellate levels, respectively. Chapter Nine discusses how the clinics have dealt with implementation challenges. Chapter Ten notes successes and areas of promise in the clinics. Finally, Chapter Eleven draws lessons learned from the process evaluation.

The monograph contains two sizable appendixes, available online (see Davis et al., 2009). Appendix A contains the individual site reports for each of the clinics visited. The individual site reports provide more detail from each site on issues discussed in the body of the monograph. Appendix B presents a detailed description of victims' rights legislation and case law in the eight NCVLI clinic states, which is summarized in Chapter Four. A third appendix, Appendix C, details the interview topics.

CHAPTER TWO

The Development of Crime Victims' Rights in the United States

Legal rights for crime victims have been developed and expanded in the past three decades. These rights have transformed the relationship between the crime victim and the criminal-justice system, as victims gained the rights to be informed, present, and heard during the criminal- and juvenile-justice processes. This change has been driven largely by crime victims and survivors, with the support of advocacy organizations, leaders within the criminal-justice field, and policymakers.

The adoption of victims' rights accelerated in the early 1980s following the release of the final report of President Ronald Reagan's Task Force on Victims of Crime (1982). That task force had been assembled to investigate the treatment of victims by the criminal-justice system. Its 1982 final report defined an agenda for bringing a balance between the rights of defendants and victims. It called for increased participation by victims throughout criminal-justice proceedings and restitution in all cases in which victims suffer financial loss.

At the same time the task force was undertaking its work, Congress was developing legislation to provide protections for victims at the federal level. The 1982 Victim and Witness Protection Act (Pub. L. 97-291) authorized victim restitution and the use of victims' impact statements at sentencing in federal cases. It also required the attorney general to issue guidelines for the development of further policies regarding victims and witnesses of crimes. Soon after, the 1984 Victims of Crime Act (VOCA) (Pub. L. 98-473) implemented more of the task force's recommendations on victim compensation and assistance. This second act by Congress redistributed monies levied from federal offenders to states, funding local aid to victims ("Constitutionalizing Crime Victim Rights," 1997; Smith and Hillenbrand, 1999, pp. 247–249).

In 1990, Congress passed the Victims' Rights and Restitution Act (Pub. L. 101-647), giving crime victims in federal cases the right to notification of court proceedings and the right to attend them, the right to notice of changes in a defendant's detention status, the right to consult with prosecutors, and the right to protection against offender aggression.

In 1994, the Violent Crime Control and Law Enforcement Act (Pub. L. 103-322) gave victims in federal cases the right to speak at sentencing hearings, made restitution mandatory in sexual-assault cases, and expanded funding for local victim services. Rights for federal crime victims were further strengthened as part of the Antiterrorism and Effective Death Penalty Act of 1996 (Pub. L. 104-132), and the Victim Rights Clarification Act of 1997 (Pub. L. 105-6).

Then in 2004, Congress passed the Crime Victims' Rights Act (CVRA) as part of the Justice for All Act of 2004 (Pub. L. 108-405). The CVRA generally strengthened the rights of federal crime victims and transferred them from Title 42, the Public Health and Welfare Code, to Title 18, the Crimes and Criminal Procedure code, elevating their profile within the federal justice system. The rights protected under the CVRA include the right to be reasonably protected from the accused; the right to be informed of criminal proceedings and the custody status of the defendant; the right to be present in the courtroom; the right to be heard at proceedings involving release, plea agreement, sentencing, or parole; the right to confer with the prosecutor; the right to restitution from the defendant; the right to proceedings free from unreasonable delay; and the right to be treated with fairness, dignity, and respect.

Victims' rights at the state level also progressed dramatically during this same time period. By the early 1980s, four states had broad laws providing a range of rights to victims, eight required a victims' impact statement at sentencing, six had open parole hearings, and eight mandated restitution for victims (DOJ, 1986). The first state victims' rights legislation was largely advisory; many such laws were called "guidelines" for the treatment of victims, rather than conferring "rights."

As at the federal level, the release of the final report of the President's Task Force on Victims of Crime in 1982 spurred the states to strengthen and expand victims' rights. By the early 1990s, every state provided violent-crime victims the right to victim compensation and provided victims of serious crime with a set of legal rights, including the rights to be informed, present, and heard during the criminal-justice process and to receive restitution from the offender.[1] Many also gave victims rights to protection from the defendant, speedy trial, privacy, and other rights to fair treatment by the criminal- and juvenile-justice systems.

Along with statutory rights for victims, 32 states amended their constitutions to provide additional protection for the rights of victims. While amending a state's constitution is a cumbersome process, typically requiring multiple levels of approval by a state legislature as well as ratification by the voters, victims' advocates pursued these amendments for the additional authority they give to victims' rights. Rights protected by the constitution cannot be diminished by anything in a state's statutes, court rules, or administrative code provisions. A constitutional amendment also provides a level of permanency to the victims' rights, since they can be changed only by another cumbersome, multiyear amendment process. And constitutional rights offer a level of implied enforceability.

State victims' rights amendments generally take one of two forms. The first is a short and broad statement of rights. Colorado's amendment takes this approach:

> Any person who is a victim of a criminal act, or such person's designee, legal guardian, or surviving immediate family members if such person is deceased, shall have the right to be heard when relevant, informed, and present at all critical stages of the criminal justice process. All terminology, including the term "critical

---

[1] Every state provides rights to victims of violent felonies. Most states extend rights to victims of any felony as well as any violent misdemeanor. A few states provide rights to a victim of any crime.

> stages", shall be defined by the general assembly. (Colo. Const. art. II, §16a)

In contrast, Arizona's amendment provides a list of 12 rights, as well as a definition of *victim* and other language to guide implementation (Ariz. Const. art. II, §2.1).

Most of the state amendments mandate notification of victims concerning events in court and the parole or release of offenders, and permit victims to participate in their cases through oral or written input at sentencing. Fewer state constitutions extend other rights, such as the right to a speedy trial and the right to participate in parole proceedings or proceedings involving pretrial release.

States also began to amend their court rules of criminal procedure and evidence to incorporate the rights of victims. While victims' rights across the states are not uniform in scope or application, most victims of serious crime are entitled to basic rights under the law.

Enforceability of Crime Victims' Rights

Despite this remarkable progress in the passage of crime victims' rights, advocates have been dismayed to see that, too often, victims' rights were violated with impunity. An NIJ-funded survey of crime victims in 1998 found that, even within states with strong victims' rights legislation, many victims were not notified about key hearings and proceedings, many were not given the opportunity to be heard, and few received restitution (Kilpatrick, Beatty, and Howley, 1998). Although victims in these states generally fared better than those in states with weak victims' rights legislation, as many as one-third of victims in strong-protection states were not afforded the opportunity to exercise certain rights.

Few states—even those that have adopted constitutional amendments—provide recourse to victims when their rights are not honored. With the exception of Arizona, all states ban any civil action for damages caused by a violation of rights. State victims' rights laws also typically provide that a violation of rights will not constitute grounds for a new trial or to overturn a sentence or other disposition. Several states restrict enforceability even further, providing that the victims' bill of rights creates no cause of action against the state. In those states, the term *cause of action* is not specifically limited to actions for damages, so the language could be interpreted in some courts to bar any action to enforce the rights of victims.[2] Two states, New York and North Dakota, have legislative language providing that a violation of their victims' bills of rights gives rise to no cause of action for money damages or injunctive relief (N.Y. Exec. Law §649[2008]; N.D. Cent. Code §12.1-34-05[2008]).[3]

Only four states—Arizona, Florida, Indiana, and Texas—provide victims express legal standing through their constitution or statutes to assert their rights (Ariz. Rev. Stat. §13-4437 [2008]; Fla. Stat. §960.001[7][2008]; Ind. Code §35-40-2-1[2008]; Tex. Const. art. I, §30 [2008]). Another two—Maryland and Utah—provide a clear right for victims to seek an appeal where their rights are denied (Md. Code Ann. Crim. Proc. §11-103 [2008]; Md. Rules 8-111 and 8-204[2008]; Utah Code Ann. §77-38-11[2008]), and several others expressly allow a limited legal remedy, such as authorizing the prosecutor or a state victims' advocate to assert a victim's rights, or allowing the victim or others to seek a writ of mandamus ordering an official or agency to comply with the victims' rights law (e.g., Ala. Code §15-23-83[2008], authorizing attorney general or district attorney to assert victims' rights; Conn. Gen. Stat. §46a-13c [2008], authorizing the state victims' advocate to file a limited special appearance for the purpose of advocating for a victim's rights; N.C. Gen. Stat. §15A-840[2008],

---

2 This is not necessarily the case, however. Florida's victims' bill of rights both provides that "Nothing in this section or in the guidelines adopted pursuant to this section shall be construed as creating a cause of action against the state or any of its agencies or political subdivisions" and gives crime victims standing to assert their rights. See Fla. Stat. §960.001(5) and (7). Thus, it would seem that the intent of "cause of action" here is restricted to monetary damages, although it is not specifically stated.

3 In both of these states, however, this prohibition is limited to the general listing of rights, in both states called the Fair Treatment Standards, and does not appear to apply to other, discrete rights of victims that appear elsewhere in the code, such as the right to be heard at specific proceedings or the right to restitution.

authorizing a victim to seek a writ of mandamus enforcing the victim's rights).

At least nine states have created or designated an entity to receive and investigate reports of violations of victims' rights. These may take the form of a state ombudsman, a committee or board, a state victims' advocate or victims' rights office, or another designated office or individual.

The issue of enforceability of victims' rights came to the federal level in 2004, when Congress passed the CVRA as part of the Justice for All Act of 2004. Along with listing the rights of victims, the CVRA gave victims legal standing to enforce their rights in court and called for the creation of a mechanism to receive and investigate reports of victims' rights violations. The larger Justice for All Act also promoted the enforceability of victims' rights at the state level by authorizing funding for legal clinics to represent the rights of victims in criminal proceedings. The statute specified that funding would be provided to the OVC for the NCVLI to provide grants and assistance to lawyers to help victims of crime in court.

CHAPTER THREE

National Crime Victim Law Institute and Clinic Goals

NCVLI was established in 2000 in an effort to promote the enforcement of victims' rights as well as awareness and education in the area of crime victims' rights. According to its Web site, NCVLI was conceived as "a national resource for crime victim lawyers and victims to support the assertion and enforcement of victims' rights in criminal and civil processes" (NCVLI, undated [a]). Its mission is to promote balance and fairness in the justice system through crime victim–centered legal advocacy, education, and resource sharing. To achieve its mission, NCVLI seeks to do the following:

- Promote victims' rights, including those of underserved and marginalized victims, in the criminal- and civil-justice systems.
- Conduct, support, and promote impact litigation through NCVLI's independent participation.
- Provide support for and promote legal technical assistance to victims' attorneys and others serving victims.
- Educate primarily lawyers, judges, law students, victims, victims' advocates, the law-enforcement community, and the public.
- Reform law through model laws and protocols, public-policy advocacy, and advocacy assistance.

NCVLI hosts an annual conference on crime victims' rights law and has a membership organization, the National Alliance of Victims' Rights Attorneys (NAVRA). NAVRA is an "alliance of attorneys committed to the protection, enforcement, and advancement of crime victims' rights nationwide" (NCVLI, undated [b]). NAVRA currently has 631 members, of whom 268 are attorneys, 296 are advocates, and 67 are others interested in victims' rights. NCVLI provides NAVRA members with an email list; conference-call training on crime victims' rights issues; quarterly case updates, which are case summaries compiled by rights topic; email updates on new and noteworthy cases immediately upon the decision issuing; a weekly digest on news touching on victims' rights both domestically and internationally; a semiannual newsletter with substantive articles on victim law; a discount at NCVLI's annual conference; and access to NCVLI's brief and memorandum bank.

In 2002, to help secure enforcement of victims' rights through direct pro bono representation of victims in the criminal-justice process, the OVC within the U.S. Department of Justice (DOJ) entered into a cooperative agreement with NCVLI to establish pro bono legal clinics in several jurisdictions. The State and Federal Clinics and System Demonstration Project was created to advocate for victims' rights in criminal-justice systems and to educate legal professionals about victims' rights law. In 2004, the federal Crime Victims' Rights Act (Pub. L. 108-405) passed and included an authorization for an appropriation of funds to help protect the newly provided victims' rights, as well any substantially equivalent rights found in states, through direct representation. The first funds appropriated under this authorization came in 2005.

According to NCVLI's director, the strategy for advancing victims' rights came, in part, from the National Association for the Advancement of Colored People's (NAACP's) legal strategy against segregation. According to an authoritative book on that legal battle (Tushnet, 2004), the NAACP strategy involved both intelligent general litigation and local support. The national litigation was considered to be an ad hoc exercise, requiring flexibility and a recognition that setbacks are inevitable and part of the process. Local communities provided plaintiffs as well as political support. This seems to fit well our observations of NCVLI's strategy that combines a focused strategic litigation program that capitalizes on opportunities presented by local complainants with efforts to win the "hearts and minds" of local criminal-justice officials.

In launching the project, including establishing the victims' rights clinics, NCVLI sought to change the legal culture with respect to its treatment of crime victims such that the system would see the victim as a participant with legally cognizable rights. One vehicle for doing this was providing direct legal representation to individual victims. By giving victims attorneys, NCVLI hoped that it could increase enforcement of rights in those particular cases. But it also hoped that these cases would establish precedent that would lead to enforcement of rights in future cases and that the mere presence of victims' attorneys in some cases and trainings held for court officials would result in an increased compliance with and enforcement of victims' rights by prosecutors, judges, and police officers in all cases—not just in the cases in which victims were represented by attorneys.

Moreover, initiating strategic litigation at the appellate level was designed to expand judicial enforcement of victims' rights in state and federal court and create precedent. This could happen through published, or even unpublished, appeals court opinions. In NCVLI's view, when victims' rights are litigated well, even losing cases at the appellate level could result in long-term gain; cases that are lost can clarify the law and show what victims' rights statutes actually mean. The new clarity may impel legislators to enact new and broader statutes. In addition, change of the criminal-justice culture could be achieved through changes to court rules.

The individual clinics share the same goals as NCVLI. An examination of their funding proposals to NCVLI revealed that all espoused the goals of providing effective representation to crime victims and educating criminal-justice professionals—judges, prosecutors, police officers, and victims' advocates—on victims' rights issues; assessing victims' crime-related needs and making appropriate referrals; and establishing a network of pro bono attorneys. The Utah clinic listed training law students as one of its goals.

Although the goals of NCVLI and the state clinics are congruent, there is a difference in emphasis. NCVLI is focused on system change. NCVLI argues that it is not the number of victims represented or even the number of appellate decisions that matters, but the quality of the opinions and the extent to which they broaden the definition and enforceability of victims' rights. On site visits to state clinics, we often heard clinic staff emphasize their duty to their clients. For example, while a clinic attorney might want to appeal a lower court's decision in order to get a published opinion that clarifies certain rights, he or she will respect the wishes of victims who do not want to go forward with an appeal. In deciding whether to take a case, a state clinic is likely to consider need of the victim as seriously as the potential of the case to result in an outcome that will help to change the culture. This tension between the goal of changing the legal culture and the duty to act as advocates for individual victims should not be overstated. The directors of all the clinics are intent on using the clinics and litigation to expand victims' rights, exactly as intended by NCVLI, just as NCVLI acknowledges that system-change work must always bow to the interests of the individual client. The difference is one of perspective: NCVLI staff are able to take a long view, while state clinic attorneys are "in the trenches" dealing with people who have been hurt and who have immediate needs—psychological, financial, and physical—as well as legal.

Clinic Grant Requirements

The grant programs through which NCVLI receives federal funds and subgrants them to the clinics have undergone several iterations since the beginning of the demonstration project in 2002. NCVLI received its first grant that year to develop the clinic program, and the first clinic to come on board was Arizona's in 2003, followed by Maryland, New Mexico, and South Carolina (as well as California and Missouri, which are no longer in the program) in 2004. The Arizona clinic was selected as the clinic to undertake federal work that same year. In 2005, NCVLI added the Idaho, New Jersey, and Utah clinics to the demonstration project. The demonstration project officially ended in 2009, although the clinics wrapped up their efforts prior to this date, and, since then, the clinics have been funded under additional federal grants for victims' rights enforcement, with all clinics now having the ability to do both federal and state work.

With each new federal grant and its attendant subgrants, the requirements for the clinics have changed somewhat. Core to every grant has been the requirement that the clinics provide free legal assistance to crime victims in criminal court, including motion practice.[1] Because motion practice is the core strategy for NCVLI's goal of changing the legal culture to more regularly afford victims' rights, it has also been the key requirement of all clinics from their inception. The initial grant included a requirement for the clinics to recruit, train, and use pro bono attorneys, but NCVLI has since reduced the stringency of the pro bono requirement, making it an aspect of achieving effective representation for victims rather than a separate goal and objective of the clinics. Conversely, the requirement for the clinics to help crime victims secure nonlegal support services has strengthened over the different grant versions, with the original requirement being the development of a victims' service network and more-recent grants requiring assessment of victims' needs and coordinating access to social services. Some clinics achieve this through their own in-house victims' advocates, while others do it through referrals to local victims' service providers. NCVLI subgrant funds may be used for these nonlegal support services, as long as the provision of legal services remains at the forefront of the clinics' work.

NCVLI Support for the Clinics

NCVLI supports clinic activities in a variety of ways. NCVLI technical assistance generally breaks down into three categories: general organizational development support, direct technical assistance (TA) to an individual clinic on a legal issue or upcoming training, and fostering peer support among the network of clinics and NAVRA members.

[1] The term *motion practice* refers to an attorney filing motions with the court. Motion practice is central to NCVLI's legal strategy, because it is the only way to inject victims' rights issues into the court's written records and to spur judicial decisions on victims' rights matters. While other forms of practice, such as letters to prosecutors and courts, may help individual victims and advance rights, they generally cannot create precedent and therefore do not substantially advance victim law as a field.

General Organizational Support

As an intermediary organization that passes through government grant funds, NCVLI has an essential role in ensuring that its subgrantees—the clinics—follow all federal rules and procedures for handling grant funds. This may include helping the subgrantees to set up or modify their accounting and data-tracking procedures in ways that ensure compliance with grant requirements, advising them on hiring and training new staff and setting up supervision procedures, and other types of organizational support.

Direct Legal Technical Assistance

Each legal clinic is assigned one attorney staff member at NCVLI as its primary contact for legal TA. That NCVLI attorney, together with the NCVLI program manager and executive director (also attorneys), will work with the individual clinic as much or as little as is needed, according to the experience of the clinic staff and the specific challenges being encountered. The general rule is that NCVLI holds an individual check-in call with new clinics monthly for the first six to nine months of the clinic's existence, to monitor its start-up period and ensure a solid foundation. For all clinics—new and more experienced—the assigned NCVLI attorney, program manager, and executive director are available as needed for help with legal research and guidance with preparing motions, briefs, oral arguments, and training materials.[2] According to NCVLI's director, the frequency with which the clinics take advantage of these services ranges from only the check-in calls to several times per week. Finally, NCVLI files amicus curiae briefs on important victims' rights issues in state and federal cases, sometimes in cases unrelated to the clinics and sometimes in cases in which a clinic is directly representing the victim.

Fostering Peer Support

NCVLI undertakes several activities to foster peer support and knowledge sharing among the clinics. It holds regular conference calls with

---

[2] While each clinic has an assigned attorney, the TA requests are often spread to other attorneys and law students working within NCVLI.

all clinics, during which NCVLI gives general grant guidance and the clinics share recent successes and challenges and learn from each other's experiences. The frequency of these conference calls has changed over the years since the inception of the clinics, from monthly to bimonthly to quarterly. (New clinics that need more-frequent guidance receive individual calls.) Another way in which NCVLI helps the clinics to learn from each other's work is through its *brief bank*—a collection of legal briefs filed by victims' attorneys on various victims' rights issues—that can help jump-start the drafting of a brief or legal argument by other victims' rights clinics or attorneys. NCVLI also encourages the clinics to use a clinic email list to conduct *case rounds*, in which a clinic will present a case or an issue on which it is working to the other clinics and pose questions that tap the other clinics' experience with similar cases or issues. This same list is also used to highlight successful legal and educational strategies, as well as to identify hurdles experienced.

NCVLI's signature peer-learning event, which was mentioned by nearly all clinic attorneys as being extremely helpful, is its annual clinic cluster meeting and national conference. The cluster meeting is a day-long meeting of staff from all NCVLI-funded clinics. Evaluation staff attended the cluster meetings in 2008 and 2009 and observed three principal activities: presentations by NCVLI staff to provide guidance on grant requirements and perspective on the overall victims' rights movement; presentations by the clinic attorneys to their peers on specific aspects of victims' rights practice with recent case examples; and social support and networking among the clinic staff. Because the clinics are dispersed geographically, this is generally the one time each year that the staff members of the different clinics see each other in person. Clinic staff reported that this aspect of the meeting—simply getting together with others who are engaged in the same challenging work—is one of the most important to them, as it helps to keep them grounded and motivated in the difficult work they are doing. The cluster meeting, which is exclusively for the clinics, is followed by a two-day victims' rights conference that is open to anyone and generally draws an audience of more than 125 attorneys, victims' advocates, counselors, and others interested in victims' rights laws and their enforcement. The clinic attorneys regularly present sessions at the conference, along with other presenters who are national experts in different aspects of victims' rights.

CHAPTER FOUR

Victims' Rights Developments in Clinic States

Each of the eight clinic states has a long history of support for crime victims' rights. All have protected the rights of victims through amendments to their state constitutions and have adopted statutory victims' bills of rights. Some have worked steadily to expand victims' rights laws beyond the amendments and bills of rights, incorporating victims' rights wherever appropriate throughout their criminal procedure and corrections codes, in their court rules of criminal procedure and evidence, and in their administrative codes. Arizona, Maryland, and Utah provide the best examples of this evolution in victims' rights.

Certain developments in victims' rights in the clinic states have directly affected the ability of clinics to represent victims; others have affected the issues the clinics have addressed.

Victim Standing

One significant area of legal development—and one that directly affects the work of the clinics—has been the issue of crime victims' legal standing to assert their rights.[1] Crime victims do not automatically have legal standing in criminal proceedings, since they are not a party

[1] The federal legislation authorizing funding through OVC for the support of victims' rights clinics restricts that funding to those serving victims in "Federal jurisdictions, and in States and tribal governments that have laws substantially equivalent to the provisions of chapter 237 of title 18, United States Code." Chapter 237 is the CVRA, which not only sets out the legal rights of victims but also provides that victims or their lawful representatives and the federal prosecutor have the ability to assert those rights. The CVRA also permits the

to the action. Instead, criminal actions represent a contest between the state and the defendant. However, some form of legal standing is essential if victims are to be able to assert their rights in the criminal case. What's more, legal representatives—in this case, the clinics—are limited by the scope of legal standing given to the victims themselves. Therefore, crime victims' legal standing underpins the viability of the legal clinics.

While most states—even most states with funded victims' rights clinics—do not have express victim standing to enforce their rights, standing can be implied where those rights are guaranteed by constitution. Since the U.S. Supreme Court's ruling in 1803 in the case of *Marbury v. Madison*, it has been understood that, "where a specific duty is assigned by law, and individual rights depend upon the performance of that duty, it seems equally clear, that the individual who considers himself injured, has a right to resort to the laws of his country for a remedy" (*Marbury v. Madison*, 5 U.S. 137, 1803). While this is a contestable legal argument, it has been used by advocates as a basis for inferring victim standing.

Arizona

Of all the clinic states, Arizona has the clearest law providing crime victims legal standing to assert their rights. Legislation adopted to implement the state's victims' rights amendment in 1991 gave victims standing and provided that victims could be represented by private counsel. That statute has been expanded over the years and, today, provides that

> The victim has standing to seek an order, to bring a special action or to file a notice of appearance in an appellate proceeding seeking to enforce any right or to challenge an order denying any right guaranteed to victims under the [constitutional amendment], any

---

victim to seek a writ of mandamus from the U.S. Court of Appeals to enforce the victim's rights.

Thus, all clinic states, in securing federal funding, had to demonstrate that they had enforceable victims' rights. Indeed, crime victims' standing to assert their rights is key to the functioning of the clinics, since they would be powerless to assist victims who had no legal ability to assert their rights in court.

> implementing legislation or court rules. In asserting any right, the victim has the right to be represented by personal counsel at the victim's expense. (Ariz. Rev. Stat. §13-4437)

The statute also gives the prosecutor the right to assert the victim's rights and gave victims the right to bring a civil action for damages where the victim's rights were intentionally violated.

In 2005, the law was extended to require that the victim's attorney, if present, must be included in all bench conferences, chamber meetings, and sessions with the trial court where those proceedings involve a victim's constitutional right. The legislature also gave the victim standing to file a notice of appearance in an appellate proceeding, at the juvenile or criminal level, seeking to enforce any right or challenge an order denying any victim's right. And it gave victims who file a notice of appearance the right to respond to a request for an extension of time to file a brief in any appellate or other postconviction proceeding in a capital case.

This law has been further extended. In 2006, the legislature provided that failure to comply with a victim's right is grounds for the victim to request a reexamination proceeding within ten days of the violation or with leave for the court with good cause shown. The court must reconsider any decision arising from the proceeding at which the victim's rights were not protected. This right to reexamination, however, does not give the victim grounds to seek to set aside a conviction after trial or provide grounds to seek a new trial.

In 2007, Arizona law was further amended to give victims the right to receive, at no charge, the minute entry or portion of the record of any court proceeding reasonably necessary for pursuing their rights.

Maryland

Maryland's journey toward legal standing has also evolved over time. The Maryland legislature first gave victims of violent crime the right to seek the appeal of the denial of certain of their rights in 1993. It provided that

> Although not a party to a criminal proceeding, the *victim* of the violent crime for which the defendant is charged has the right

> to file an application for leave to appeal to the Court of Special Appeals from an interlocutory or final order that denies or fails to consider [the rights to be informed of their rights, to be present, to be heard, and to receive an order of restitution]. (Md. Code Ann. Crim. Proc. §11-103)

Since that time, due to the efforts of the Maryland clinic's parent organization (the Maryland Crime Victims' Resource Center) and, indirectly, through the work of the clinic, victim standing has been further developed. The legislature extended the statutory right to seek appeal to victims of violent offenses committed by juvenile offenders. Court rules facilitating the right to seek an appeal (Md. Rules 8-111 and 8-204) were adopted. And, perhaps most significantly, a court rule was adopted that authorizes a victim's attorney to enter a formal appearance in a criminal or juvenile case to represent the rights of the victim (Md. Rule 1-326).

Utah

Utah included various measures victims could take to secure their rights as part of the implementing legislation adopted for its victims' rights amendment in 1994. These measures include the right to "bring an action for declaratory relief or for a writ of mandamus defining or enforcing the rights of victims and the obligations of government entities under this chapter," the right to petition to file an amicus brief in any case affecting crime victims, and the right to appeal adverse rulings on these actions. In 1995, this statute was expanded to permit victims to appeal adverse rulings "on a motion or request brought by a victim of a crime or a representative of a victim of a crime" (Utah Code §77-38-11, 2008).

This general right of victims to appeal adverse rulings relating to their rights has been affirmed by the state's Supreme Court (*State v. Casey*, 2002 UT 29, 44 P.3d 756, 762, 2002). (The victim in that case was represented by NCVLI staff and Paul Cassell, one of the founders of the Utah clinic and author of the state's amendment and implementing legislation.)

South Carolina

South Carolina does not provide crime victims express legal standing to assert their rights. However, in the victims' rights amendment to its constitution, it does provide that victims' rights

> may be subject to a writ of mandamus, to be issued by any justice of the Supreme Court or circuit court judge to require compliance by any public employee, public agency, the State, or any agency responsible for the enforcement of the rights and provisions of these services. (S.C. Const. art. I, §24)

The constitution is silent on the question of who has the authority to seek such a writ.

Attorneys' ability to represent victims with regard to their legal rights was recently affirmed by the South Carolina attorney general. In 2007, the clinic was involved in a criminal domestic-violence case, and the solicitor (prosecutor) failed to notify the victim's attorney (the clinic director at the time) of a bond hearing for the defendant. After being contacted by the clinic's parent organization, a state senator requested an opinion from the attorney general regarding the solicitor's obligation to give notice of judicial proceedings to attorneys who have filed a formal notice of appearance on behalf of a crime victim. In his written opinion, the attorney general reviewed the statutory requirements regarding victim notification and the legislature's intent that victims' rights be protected to the same degree as the rights of defendants and noted that the state constitution protected victims' right to be informed. The attorney general ruled that, where a victim's attorney has filed a formal notice of appearance, the attorney should be provided written notice contemporaneously with the prosecution and defense of all court hearings and that, if an attorney files notice with law-enforcement and prosecuting agencies that also have a responsibility to notify victims, those agencies should also attempt to send notice to the attorney as well as to the victims (S.C. Attorney General Opinion No. 07-034).

The remaining states have no statutory or constitutional provisions expressly providing victims a general or limited ability to assert their rights.

New Jersey

New Jersey law does not expressly provide legal standing to victims to enforce their rights. However, the courts have considered crime victims' actions relating to their rights. In 1997, a judge in a division of the appellate court specifically held that the victims' rights amendment "provides victims with specific rights, and that these rights carry with them standing for a victim to voice their concerns and protect their constitutional rights" (*In re K.P.*, 709 A.2d 315, 321, N.J. Super. Ct. Ch. Div., 1997). In its decision, the court noted a prior New Jersey Supreme Court case that referenced the voters' expression of support for that state's victims' rights amendment in upholding one of the statutory rights that implemented it (*State v. Muhammad*, 145 N.J. 23, 678 A.2d 164, 1996). Although there has been no appellate case denying victim standing and one that upholds it, the New Jersey clinic considers the issue unsettled and is hoping to see victims explicitly granted standing in a future revision of the statutory victims' bill of rights.

New Mexico

New Mexico's laws are also silent on the ability of victims to assert their rights. In fact, as noted earlier, New Mexico's statute provides that violation of the victim's rights does not create any cause of action against an official or agency responsible for enforcement of those rights. Even so, the New Mexico clinic has been successful in obtaining an *unreported* New Mexico Supreme Court order granting standing to the victim in the case at issue (*Nasci v. Pope*, No. 29,878, N.M., 2006). The language of the order was limited. However, when considered in conjunction with the pleadings of the victim, defendant, and an amicus brief from the state criminal-defense attorneys' association, the statutory language providing that violation of rights creates "no cause of action" in the statutory enabling legislation was determined to only refer to *monetary* causes of action. This is because action by the legislature to refuse victim standing would exceed its authority under the separation of powers under the New Mexico Constitution—as standing to assert constitutional rights is a matter for the courts to determine rather than the legislature. The result was that victims have standing to assert a claim for injunctive relief under the Victim's Rights Constitutional Amendment (N.M. Const. art. II, §24). Ordinarily, unpublished orders have no precedential value in other cases. However, because the New Mexico Supreme Court considered the issue en banc and was unanimous in its decision, the clinic considers this order a monumental step, and it has actively and successfully made use of it to promote victim standing in trial courts.

Colorado

Colorado's laws, too, are silent on victim standing. The Colorado Supreme Court has addressed a limited question of victim standing. In the case of *Gansz v. State* (888 P.2d 256, 1995), a victim sought to appeal the dismissal of criminal charges. The supreme court ruled that the victim did not have standing to appeal a dismissal of criminal charges. Importantly, this action was outside of the scope of the crime victims' rights laws. "There is no statutory right to be heard at a hearing on a district attorney's motion to dismiss criminal charges." The state supreme court has not ruled, generally, on the victim's ability to assert his or her legal rights.

Idaho

Idaho's laws make no mention of victims' ability to assert their rights, and there has been no appellate-level consideration of the victim's standing in that state.

Laws That Further Crime Victims' Representation in Criminal Matters

While laws providing victims the authority to assert their rights are most important to the functioning of the clinics, a few states have also seen legal developments that financially support or in other ways facilitate the work of the clinics.

Maryland created a source of financial support for the clinic or other efforts to represent crime victims. It amended its restitution law to provide that restitution collected for a victim who cannot be located will be deposited into a fund to provide grants for victims' legal representation (Md. Code. Crim. Proc. §11-919, 2008; Md. Code Comm. Law §17-317, 2008).

New Jersey added new duties to the victim-witness rights information program, requiring that victims be informed about their constitutional and statutory rights and about obtaining legal advice or representation, and requiring the information program to conduct trainings for attorneys (N.J. Stat. §52:4B-42, 2008). The state also amended its victims' compensation law to authorize the compensation program to reimburse the victim for attorneys' fees for legal assistance in any legal matter relating to the offense. There is a cap on the amount of such fees that can be claimed (N.J. Stat. §52:4B-8, 2008). Previously, the law limited compensation for attorneys fees related to legal representation of the victim on matters regarding the compensation claim itself—for example, appealing the denial of a claim (N.J. Stat. §52:4B-8, 2006).

Crime Victims' Right to Privacy

Another area of development in victims' rights common to several of the states relates to the victims' right to privacy. These developments have opened up a new area for legal representation of victims.

Two states—Arizona and Utah—have taken on the issue of abuse of blank subpoenas by defense counsel to request the private records of victims, usually including counseling records. In 2006, Arizona passed a statute prohibiting the use of blank subpoenas to access the records of a victim, providing that records relating to recovered memories may be subpoenaed only if certain conditions are met, and giving victims the right to be notified and heard at any proceeding involving a subpoena of their records (Ariz. Stat. §13-4071, 2008).

Utah passed similar restrictions through amendments to its court rules in 2007 (Utah R. Crim. P. 14). The revised rule requires that, before a victim's records can be requested, the court must first hold a hearing and determine that the defendant is entitled to such records. The revision also requires that the prosecutor and any attorney representing the victim be informed of the request for subpoena. Additional protections are included. Notably, an advisory-committee note to the rule amendment states that the addition of this new subsection is

> intended . . . to adopt a procedure consistent with current applicable law that balances a victim's state constitutional right "[t]o be treated with fairness, respect, and dignity, and to be free from harassment and abuse throughout the criminal justice process," with a defendant's constitutional right to due process. Requiring a defendant to apply to the court for the production of a victim's records ensures that a victim or his or her representative will have an opportunity to assert any privileges or reasons why the records should not be subject to either release or *in camera* review. (Utah R. Crim. P. 14, advisory committee's note)

Other provisions addressing victims' privacy have also been adopted in clinic states during the time the clinics have been functioning. Arizona passed a law protecting victims' information in publicly accessible records relating to the case, with an exception for the victim's name and the location of the crime (Ariz. Stat. §13-4434, 2008). Colorado made victims' compensation records confidential (Colo. Stat. §24-72-204, 2008). Idaho protected the social security numbers of persons contained in court records (Idaho Misd. Crim. Proc. R. 2.1). Maryland amended court rules to prevent remote electronic access to information pertaining to victims and nonparty witnesses in criminal cases and to shield information in court records pertaining to a person who sought a protective order or who is a victim of domestic violence (Md. Rules 16-1008, 16-1009). New Jersey added an administrative code provision that denied convicted offenders access to a government record containing the personal information about a victim or the victim's family (N.J.A.C. §10A:31-6.5). South Carolina required that victims' information be kept confidential by custodial authorities (S.C. Code §16-3-1535, 2008). Utah created a court rule addressing the selective closing of court records relating to victims and witnesses for safety and privacy reasons (Utah R. Judicial Admin. 4-202). And Colorado, Idaho, Maryland, and New Mexico all created address-confidentiality programs that provide alternative official addresses for domestic-violence victims and certain others (Colo. Stat. §§24-21-201–214, 2008; Idaho

Code §§19-5701–5708, 2008; Md. Code. Family Law §§4-519–530, 2008; N.M. Stat. §40-13-11, 2008).

Other Changes

All of the clinic states continued their general drive to expand the rights of victims, extending the right to be informed to additional proceedings and events, clarifying the right to restitution and improving the process for collection, extending the victims' rights at parole, and increasing the rights of victims of juvenile offenders. These changes are detailed in Appendix B (see Davis et al., 2009).

CHAPTER FIVE

Clinic Operations

The NCVLI clinics work to promote observance of victims' rights by representing victims in individual cases and by working to change the legal culture through example, training, and appellate decisions and court rules that acknowledge victims' rights. When they become aware of a potential rights violation, the first step may be to place a call to a criminal-justice official to see whether the condition can be easily remedied. For example, they may try to convince police to file a case with the court or to convince a prosecutor to advance a trial date. Or they may ask a prosecutor to oppose a defense motion to order a victim to release medical records. Clinic attorneys also file motions in trial courts on behalf of their clients. In some states, clinic attorneys have filed motions to amend a plea to include restitution or other conditions based on statutory rights. Other attorneys have filed writs with appeals courts to get victims admitted into the courtroom after they were denied the right to be present by a trial-court judge. Finally, clinic attorneys work at the appellate level to seek published rulings that clarify or expand the scope of victims' rights on critical issues, such as victim standing and privacy.

While clinics share these common interests and activities, their ways of going about their work differ in some important respects. In this chapter, we discuss differences in the ways in which clinics are structured and how they operate. Differences along these dimensions have potential implications for the number and geographic diversity of cases that clinics handle, sources of client referrals, types of cases handled, and funding sustainability.

Type of Business Model

There is great diversity in the way in which clinics have been structured. Clinics we have visited have ranged in their organizational aegis from being housed within victim-service programs to being located within a law school to being one component within a full-service law firm. Each of these arrangements has implications for how the clinics function.

Law Clinic Model

Two clinics are formally affiliated with law schools. The Idaho clinic, as one of eight clinical programs at the University of Idaho College of Law, receives considerable benefits from the law school, including office and classroom space, use of the office manager and financial manager for the general clinic program, travel support, and supplemental funding. Under the direction of a supervising attorney, third-year law students registered for the three-credit clinic course represent victims. Since the students serve the clinic for a semester or an academic year at best, the supervising attorney's involvement is essential to continuity with the cases and clients. As a component of the law school, the clinic's first priority is educating students by exposing them to litigation, and its secondary mission is to ensure access to justice. This is a clear distinction from the victim focus and interest in helping with all of victims' needs that are the aims of most of the clinics.

The Arizona clinic, while not technically a law-school clinic, is affiliated with Arizona State University College of Law, where the founder teaches a class. Most of the students in the class volunteer for the clinic in order to receive extra credit for the class. The class is not qualified as a true clinic by the law school because the students do not directly represent clients. Rather, they assist the clinic's two contract attorneys by conducting legal research. In contrast to the Idaho clinic, the Arizona clinic emphasizes full representation of its clients, including a social worker as well as an attorney in a team approach. The team generally accompanies victims to all court proceedings. Staff emphasize that, once they enter into a representation agreement, they stick with the client even absent any victims' rights problems.

There are several advantages of the law-school clinic model. First, the connection with a university law school provides some stature to programs that they might not have if they were independent programs. Second, the use of free student labor potentially allows clinics to take on a much larger case load than would otherwise be possible on a fixed budget. Finally, while it is unlikely that students who participate in a clinic will take on victims' rights work as their primary vocation, they will take their knowledge of victims' rights and use it in their jobs as prosecutors, public defenders, guardians ad litem, or advocates for victims in civil cases.

Statewide Victim-Service Provider Model

Three of the clinics are under the umbrella of statewide victim-service providers. Perhaps the clearest example is the Maryland clinic, which resides within the Maryland Crime Victims' Resource Center (MCVRC), an organization that takes a full-service approach to victim assistance and serves victims of all types of crime. The clinic shares general staff and overhead costs with MCVRC, including rent, utilities, equipment, and supplies. MCVRC staff conducts client intakes, ensuring that each client receives the unique set of services he or she needs. Clients are referred to caseworkers within MCVRC or to social-service agencies throughout the state that can address their specific needs. In addition, social workers and staff attorneys help clients to understand their legal rights and educate clients on what they can expect during each stage of the legal process. While assessing victims' needs, intake staff note whether there are restitution or other potential victims' rights issues, and clients with rights issues are referred to the clinic.

The South Carolina victims' rights clinic has a slightly looser relationship with its sponsoring victim-advocacy organization. The clinic is housed within the South Carolina Victim Assistance Network (SCVAN), a statewide victim-advocacy organization that provides training, referrals, and direct service. While SCVAN provides administrative support and grant management as well as some outreach efforts, the clinic's director is solely responsible for all legal matters handled by the clinic. Intake on clinic cases is not conducted through the parent organization, as is the case in Maryland. However, like the Maryland clinic, the South Carolina clinic benefits from being nested within a victim-service organization. Victims seeking help from SCVAN who have legal issues are referred to the clinic. Conversely, clinic clients in need of additional services can easily access them through SCVAN's services and network.

The fledgling Colorado clinic is also based within a state network of victim-service providers, the Colorado Organization for Victim Assistance (COVA). Like the South Carolina clinic, the Colorado clinic shares offices and some administrative staff with its parent organization but maintains a separate intake process.

The statewide victim-service provider model has several arguments in its favor. Sharing intake, office, and administrative costs with a host organization keeps clinic costs down. Typically, the host organization is well established in the victim-service field and lends the clinic stature that it would otherwise have to earn from scratch, as well as invaluable connections through its board of directors and other contacts. These connections can help get the word out quickly and help bring in referrals. Moreover, in some cases, the host organization is able to engage in lobbying efforts—forbidden to the clinics on federal dollars—that build on clinic appeals cases to improve legislation.

Other Partnership Models

The Arizona clinic is under the umbrella of the Arizona Voice for Crime Victims (AVCV) and has no separate legal or organizational identity. AVCV is not a victim-service organization but rather an advocacy organization that, in addition to operating the clinic, advocates for improvements to victims' rights at the state level in Arizona. This relationship has been very beneficial to furthering Arizona's extensive legal rights for victims, as the clinic cannot conduct legislative advocacy with its federal funding but it can make AVCV aware of issues that arise in its cases, and AVCV then undertakes legislative advocacy with private funding.

The Utah and New Mexico clinics are housed within local, crime-specific, victim-serving organizations (a sexual-assault program and a drunk driving–prevention and victim-service program, respectively) and benefit from inexpensive office space. The New Mexico clinic is headed by the executive director of the DWI Resource Center, which employs a part-time staff attorney for clinic work. Although the Utah clinic may get occasional referrals from its landlord, there is no formal coordination between the work of the clinic and the work of the host sexual-assault agency.

Independent Law-Firm Model

Only the New Jersey clinic is based within a private law firm founded by the clinic director. The clinic director dedicates his full-time efforts to victims' rights cases. NCVLI funds cover the salaries of the director and an assistant. The director is partnered with two attorneys with whom he runs a full-service law firm. The two other attorneys handle real-estate law, matrimonial issues, and other civil cases, while each dedicates 25 hours per week to victims' rights work on a pro bono basis. This continues the original New Jersey model in which—before federal funding—proceeds of the law firm were used to fund victims' rights work. Eventually, the center director hopes that monies brought in from settlements won by the law firm's civil-litigation case load will be able to sustain the victims' rights work.

There are at least two advantages to this arrangement. One is that, if the director's vision is fulfilled, there is a clear path to independence from grant funding toward a stable source of permanent funding. The other is that the New Jersey clinic has been able to sustain a caseload far in excess of the other clinics, in spite of the fact that it has the geographically most dispersed caseload of all the clinics.

Use of Pro Bono Attorneys and Student Help

Although every clinic has made an effort to train pro bono attorneys and refer cases to them, we have heard many reservations from the clinic directors about the use of pro bono attorneys. Most clinic directors argued that pro bono attorneys seldom have the knowledge, commitment, or availability to be of significant help. The most strident objection came from the New Mexico clinic. Before the New Mexico Supreme Court recognizing standing, the clinic did not feel that it was wise to let other attorneys control the litigation. Even now that the New Mexico Supreme Court has recognized victim standing, the clinic staff is concerned that other attorneys will not adequately protect victims. The clinic's cardinal rule is, "First, do no further harm (to victims)," and it felt that involving pro bono attorneys might jeopardize that principle. One concern mentioned was that the outside attorneys may put their own egos ahead of the needs of the victim and that they will "revictimize the victim in the hope of saving them." Another concern, based on prior experience with pro bono attorneys, was that these attorneys would give paying clients priority over nonpaying clients. This was summed up in the remark, "You get what you pay for."

The New Jersey clinic director also has reservations about using pro bono attorneys. However, the clinic has successfully used a few pro bono attorneys who are acquaintances of the director to handle cases in disparate parts of the state. This may be part of the reason that the clinic has been able to open up a large number of cases throughout the state. The clinic also uses occasional student interns in an administrative capacity.

The Maryland clinic has taken an intermediate stance on the pro bono issue. It uses a small panel of pro bono attorneys to handle mostly collateral civil cases (e.g., estate, housing, or creditor issues), which fall outside the scope of clinic funding. The clinic also uses pro bono attorneys to help to collect restitution and to aid in writing amicus briefs for appellate cases. The clinic finds that using pro bono attorneys in this way avoids some of the problems associated with using pro bono attorneys in criminal cases—insufficient knowledge of victims' rights issues and criminal procedure, extensive need for training, and schedules that did not permit them to make necessary court appearances in clinic cases on short notice. Law courses taught by the clinic director ensure a supply of law-student interns who help clinic attorneys with case research and assist other clinic staff with intake and administrative tasks.

Other clinics, while acknowledging limitations, have more fully embraced the concept of free help. The Utah clinic has been assisted by three pro bono attorneys representing victims in court. Two of those were identified by actively calling around in each judicial district to try to identify an attorney willing and able to take the cases. The third pro bono attorney is a retired prosecutor, who, after initially acting as a pro bono attorney, now works as a part-time contract attorney for the clinic. Moreover, the clinic plans to expand its use of pro bono attorneys through targeted recruiting—reaching out to victims' advocates for the names of potential pro bono attorneys. The clinic is developing a free continuing legal education (CLE) course for attorneys in exchange for their taking one victim's case within the year following the training. (Some of the other clinics have also offered CLE courses for pro bono attorneys.) The Utah clinic also has a very active intern program. Each semester, it recruits two to four law-student interns from nearby law schools, as well as four interns over the summer. Interns contribute 100–200 hours per semester (typically one full day per week).

The South Carolina clinic is proud of its success at implementing a pro bono attorney network. Early directors of the clinic used personal contacts with lawyers across the state to develop the pro bono attorney pool. Currently the clinic has a pool of 13 pro bono attorneys who handled 18 percent of the cases the clinic opened in 2007. The clinic reports that the pool is of high quality and well placed geographically around the state. Pro bono attorneys have been especially helpful in working with clients in areas that are more distant from the clinic's offices. Pro bono attorneys take cases from start to finish. As the program grows, the clinic sees the role of pro bono attorneys expanding to help manage a growing caseload. The clinic is likely to seek the help of pro bono attorneys in cases in distant counties, where it would be difficult for clinic staff to make an appearance in court, or in cases involving relatively simple victims' rights issues (for example, the ability to offer a victim's impact statement). The clinic also tends to use pro bono attorneys in cases in which there are civil legal issues that clinic staff is not allowed to address. This situation works well, since the pro bono attorneys are permitted to collect a fee for the civil legal assistance while representing the victims in their criminal cases free of charge. A change currently under consideration to a requirement that all lawyers in South Carolina take appointments referred by the court would count pro bono work on behalf of victims as credit toward their state requirements.

We have already discussed in the preceding section the benefit that the Arizona and Idaho clinics receive from student help as a result of their law-school affiliations. The models differ—in Idaho, students represent victims in court, while, in Arizona, their efforts are confined to conducting legal research to assist clinic attorneys. Both applications of student help can reduce the costs of running victims' rights clinics. Idaho has not found a need for pro bono attorneys beyond the law students, as its caseload has remained small to date. Arizona does make limited use of a few trusted pro bono attorneys.

NCVLI has developed a circumscribed view of the utility of pro bono attorneys to contribute to the state clinics. Where once pro bono attorneys were envisioned as the long-term solution to victims' rights enforcement, now the NCVLI director sees pro bono attorneys as helpful in a more limited fashion. From a system-change perspective, they often are unable to get up to speed in time for cases capable of pushing forward the victims' rights agenda. The NCVLI director believes that pro bono attorneys are best used in cases in which victims' rights issues are less complex—for example, in arguing for restitution for victims.

If an appropriate model is used, there are obvious benefits to using pro bono or student help in order to leverage the relatively small budgets on which clinics operate. The Utah plan to develop a course to train private attorneys who are seriously interested in victims' rights work should remove two of the objections to the use of pro bono attorneys: Taking the course will ensure that volunteers are both interested and satisfactorily trained in victims' rights law.

We learned that there are hard limits on what can be expected by using free help, whether it be in the form of pro bono attorneys, law students, or interns. We believe that each has its place, and all clinics employ at least one of these resources. There may be room for law students to play a significant role in litigation activities—this idea has not been well tested. Also, pro bono attorneys who are exceptional in their interest, time commitments, and training may, in rare cases, be able to accept responsibility for litigating some cases in counties that are inaccessible to clinics. With those possible exceptions, however, we conclude that free sources of help can play a significant support role for clinics but are not a substitute for litigators trained in victims' rights law and committed to the work of the clinic.

Addressing Victims' Nonlegal Needs

While their primary focus has always been on addressing violations of clients' legal rights, all of the clinics also have developed a focus that includes addressing all of victims' crime-related needs, either directly or through referrals to other service providers. This orientation is clearest in the two clinics that are under the umbrella of statewide victim-service providers. As discussed in the preceding section, in the Maryland clinic, the director of services of the parent organization meets with the victims' advocates and the clinic's legal staff weekly to develop service plans for each client. We also noted that, in the South Carolina clinic, clinic clients in need of additional services can easily access them through the parent organization's network of service providers. The Utah clinic receives many referrals from advocates for victim clients who already are connected with service providers, and the clinic itself has a VOCA-funded victims' advocate on staff. In Arizona, every case is assigned both an attorney and a social worker, who is responsible for accompanying victims in court, providing emotional support, and ensuring that the victims are connected with any nonlegal services they need. The New Mexico and Idaho clinics have developed extensive referral networks.

Perhaps surprisingly, the most holistic approach is taken by the New Jersey clinic, which is not affiliated with any victim-service provider. Like other clinics, the New Jersey clinic aids victims in getting help with emotional and practical problems stemming from crime, aiding victims in filing applications for state compensation and referring them to a network of trusted therapists experienced in dealing with victimization issues and to other service providers as needed. In addition to attending to victims' nonlegal needs, the New Jersey clinic's holistic approach also encompasses handling civil issues for clients as well as violations of victims' rights in criminal proceedings. The two types of cases are mutually reinforcing. According to the director,

> A lawyer does not wear one hat. I see that as one of the biggest weaknesses out there. You can't [parse] the issues with your client. If you're the victims' rights lawyer, you're their lawyer on everything to do with the victimization. You can't say "I don't do that."

The New Jersey clinic is unique in providing both civil and criminal legal help to victims, on top of emotional support, advocacy, and referrals.

The fact that the clinics have concerned themselves with the totality of client needs—not just the potential value of cases in litigating rights issues—highlights the way in which the clinics' and NCVLI's approaches complement one another. Clinic attorneys appropriately act as client advocates for many crime-related needs. NCVLI, meanwhile, maintains its focus on changing the legal landscape and keeping an eye out for the cases that are likely to push its reform agenda significantly ahead.

CHAPTER SIX

Outreach and Sources of Clients

In this chapter, we discuss variations between clinics in recruitment methods and implications for referral sources, number of cases and types of cases represented, and types of victims' rights issues with which they deal. To its credit, NCVLI has not insisted on a single model for the state clinics. As discussed in Chapter Five, there are substantial variations in business models adopted by the clinics and in their use of pro bono attorneys and student help. As this chapter shows, there also are significant differences in recruitment and caseloads. The freedom that the clinics have in developing different methods allows evaluation of how differences affect clinic outcomes.

As mentioned earlier, because we did not have direct access to client files, it is likely that there are inconsistencies from site to site in how information on rights issues was coded. The reader should also note that the data presented in this section might disagree in minor ways with data presented in the individual site reports. This is due to the fact that, in order to combine data across the clinics for this chapter, we created broader categories than were used in the site reports. For example, one of the categories in the table on referral sources for the Arizona clinic (Table A.1 in Appendix A; see Davis et al., 2009) is "Parents of Murdered Children," a national organization. In the corresponding table in this chapter (Table 6.1), these cases appear in the category, "Community program/therapist/doctor."

Table 6.1
Referral Sources

Source	Md. (n = 35)	S.C. (n = 22)	N.J. (n = 50)	N.M. (n = 20)	Idaho (n = 29)	Utah (n = 85)	Ariz. (n = 27)
	Referrals from That Source (%)						
Prosecutor	11	0	16	10	24	13	44
Police victims' assistant or prosecutor victims' assistant	11	45	18	10	10	46	0
Community program/therapist/doctor	14	32	42	20	21	22	26
Web site, brochure, friend/self-referred	46	0	14	40	21	4	7
State or local official	14	14	4	5	3	0	4
Police, probation officer, corrections, private attorney	3	9	6	10	0	6	7
Solicited	0	0	0	0	12	0	0
Other	0	0	0	5[a]	9[b]	9[c]	11[d]

SOURCE: Clinic case files.

[a] Unknown (one case).

[b] Referrals from within the university system (three cases).

[c] Unknown (eight cases).

[d] Referrals from NCVLI (three cases).

Referral Sources

Table 6.1 displays sources of referral for the clinics. As the table makes clear, different clinics relied on different methods of recruitment. The Utah and South Carolina clinics received nearly half of their referrals from prosecutor victims' advocates, while all of the other clinics had less than 20 percent of case loads referred by prosecutor victims' advocates. The director of the Utah clinic, a former prosecutor, has made special efforts to reach out to prosecutors. Prosecutor referrals are especially common in cases in which the defense is seeking private records of the victim. It is interesting to note that staff of the South Carolina clinic did not name prosecutors as a major source of referral in our interviews and, in fact, indicated that there had been some friction between former clinic attorneys and prosecutors in the past. Staff did report that they conducted 27 training sessions for prosecutors in the second year of the project.

The Maryland and New Mexico clinics had a plurality of referrals from their Web sites, brochures, and word of mouth. This squares with comments of the director of the Maryland clinic, who noted during our site visit that the clinic received many referrals from its Web site. Web sites and brochures are relatively easy and inexpensive ways to garner more referrals and do not depend on the goodwill of system actors. In that respect, they may be especially useful for start-up clinics working in hostile environments. In the case of New Mexico, the clinic director told us that prosecutor advocates sometimes make "secret" referrals, asking not to be identified as having provided the referral, for fear of angering the prosecutors (their bosses). These "secret" referrals probably make up a portion of the cases listed as self-referred.

The New Jersey and South Carolina clinics received more than one in three referrals from therapists or community organizations. That makes sense, given what we learned about both of these clinics. The New Jersey clinic has a well-developed network of therapists and community organizations with which it works. The South Carolina clinic is located within a state victims' advocacy organization that consists of a network of grassroots programs.

Maryland and South Carolina—states that both have state victims' rights compliance officers—each received 14 percent of their cases from state and local officials, while other clinics received less than 5 percent from officials. (New Mexico also has a state victims' compliance officer, but she contributed only one clinic referral.) Finally, Idaho was unique in that it solicited a small proportion (7 percent) of its clients involved in high-profile cases that resulted in media coverage. This unique attempt to generate additional clients early in the clinic's career is a good example of how clinics' freedom to experiment with different methods of operation led to creative solutions to problems (in this case, low case numbers due to the clinic's rural location and newness on the scene).

Case Load Size and Composition

Clinics take different approaches to representing clients. Some accompany victims to all court hearings, while others may make only a single appearance at a critical stage in the proceedings. Additionally, some cases are more time-consuming than others (a capital murder case will require much more attorney time than a domestic-violence protective-order case, for example). Additionally, the different clinics do not necessarily have common definitions of what they count as a case. For all of these reasons, caseload is not a perfect measure of the amount of advocacy activity undertaken by the state clinics. However, in the absence of more-precise statistics, caseload does provide at least a gross measure of clinic success in gaining referrals.

Figure 6.1 shows that the largest case loads tend to be associated with clinics that are built on the work of individuals who already had stature as leaders in victims' rights in their states, likely reflecting greater acceptance by prosecutors and victims' advocates. The New Jersey, Utah, and Maryland clinics opened far more cases than the other state clinics, signing 132, 85, and 43 representation agreements in 2007, respectively. The less mature clinics (South Carolina, New Mexico, and Idaho) have not yet achieved the same level of acceptance, as gauged by the number of referrals. Each is making efforts to train prosecutors, victims' advocates, and judges about victims' rights and about the availability of legal representation for victims. These clinics are fighting battles for acceptance of the idea of legal representation for victims. Each has felt itself in an adversarial role vis-à-vis criminal-justice officials as it struggles for legitimacy, although the South Carolina clinic has made a concerted effort recently to conduct quiet diplomacy with prosecutors or law-enforcement officials where possible rather than immediately filing motions to remedy failure to observe

Figure 6.1
Cases Opened in 2007

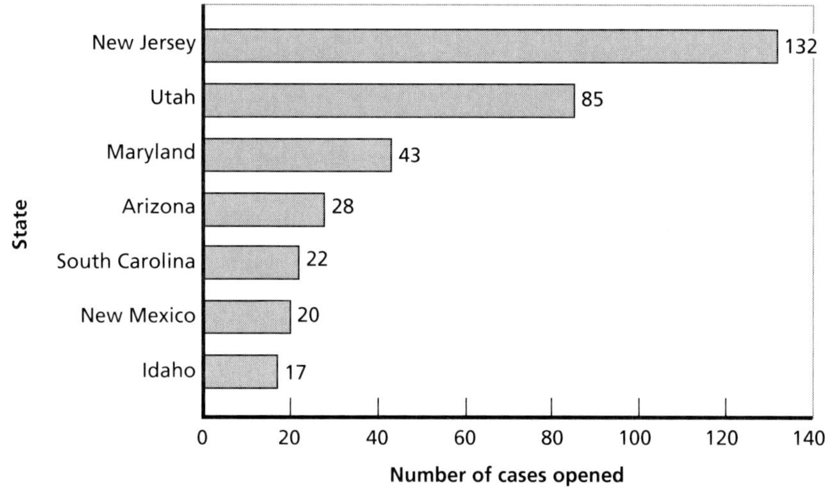

RAND *MG930-6.1*

the rights of clients.[1] The Arizona clinic has a relatively low case load because the clinic is selective in taking cases that can be used to further victims' rights issues in significant ways and because it accompanies its clients to every court proceeding—thus, each case takes a significant amount of attorney time.[2]

We noted substantial diversity on the types of crimes with which the state clinics dealt. Table 6.2 displays the types of cases in which clinics signed representation agreements with victims. Nearly two-

---

1 The South Carolina clinic believes that it achieves more success for individual victims by taking this nonconfrontational route, and NCVLI confirms that South Carolina has, indeed, achieved much through its diplomacy with prosecutors and judges. On the other hand, this approach, if taken exclusively, precludes the possibility of creating case law that furthers the victims' rights movement. There is an ongoing dialogue between NCVLI and the clinics on the merits of diplomacy versus aggressive litigation (and the continuum between these end points).

2 We note that the substantial differences between clinics in the number of clients may reflect different-size populations in each state. For example, although the Idaho clinic has the fewest clients and the New Jersey clinic the most, the rate of clients per 1,000 state population is similar.

Table 6.2
Types of Crimes in Cases in Which Representation Agreements Were Signed

	Cases (%)						
Type of Crime	**Md. (n = 43)**	**S.C. (n = 21)**	**N.J. (n = 49)**	**N.M. (n = 20)**	**Idaho (n = 29)**	**Utah (n = 85)**	**Ariz. (n = 27)**
Sexual assault	14	29	27	60	28	24	0
Domestic violence/ stalking/harassment	19	24	5	10	28	40	7
Child abuse	0	0	29	0	10	16	33
Homicide/ manslaughter	23	10	14	20	3	9	44
Assault/robbery	19	14	24	10	21	7	0
Other[a]	26	24	2	0	10	5	15

SOURCE: Clinic case files.

NOTE: Due to rounding, percentages may not sum to 100.

[a] Includes voyeurism, fraud, compensation claims, parole violations, burglary, witness tampering, victims of driving while intoxicated (DWI), and human trafficking.

thirds of the New Mexico clinic's caseload consists of sexual assaults. Relative to the other clinics, Utah's clinic handles a large proportion (40 percent) of domestic-violence and stalking cases. About three in ten of the New Jersey and Arizona clinics' case load involved child-abuse charges. Arizona also represented a far larger proportion (44 percent) of homicide victims than the other state clinics.

Rights Issues Dealt with in Cases Opened by the State Clinics

We are least certain about data on the kinds of victims' rights issues addressed in cases opened by the state clinics. Information on rights issues is most subject to differences in interpretation by the different individuals doing the coding in each of the clinics. Moreover, categorization may be influenced by the wording of particular victims' rights statutes. Table 6.3 suggests that the New Mexico clinic is more active in plea agreements than the other clinics. While all but one of the clinics had a good number of cases involving the right to be notified, present, or heard, these issues formed a majority of the caseloads of the South Carolina and Utah clinics. Maryland was the only clinic that represented a number of victims in state compensation claims.[3] The

Table 6.3
Victims' Rights Issues in Clinic Cases

	Cases (%)						
Issue	**Md. (n = 39)**	**S.C. (n = 21)**	**N.J. (n = 39)**	**N.M. (n = 20)**	**Idaho (n = 29)**	**Utah (n = 85)**	**Ariz. (n = 27)**
Charging decision	5	0	12	0	28	0	0
Plea agreement	0	5	8	35	28	0	7
Right to be notified/ present/heard	33	67	38	0	3	60	22
Speedy trial	0	5	2	5	0	5	19
Right to privacy	13	0	7	10	3	6	26
Safety from harassment/ restraining-order issues	0	10	13	5		19	19
Restitution	13	5	2	5	21	4	7
Respectful treatment	0	10	6	40	10	6	0
General/other issue[a]	36	0	12	0	7	1	0

SOURCE: Clinic case files.

NOTE: Due to rounding, percentages may not sum to 100.

[a] Includes legal representation, assistance with compensation claim, and referral for services.

[3] According to NCVLI, other clinics have helped victims with compensation claims over the years if they arose in the course of their case, but Maryland specifically marketed its services in the compensation arena and therefore did many more compensation cases, until the terms of the federal grant changed and such cases were disallowed in 2008.

Idaho clinic was more active than others in representing victims at the point of charging and on restitution issues.

Geographic Diversity of Case Load

It is very difficult for a small-budget victims' rights clinic to represent cases from all over the state. In this section, we examine the extent to which clinic caseloads are geographically diverse or concentrated in the locale where the clinics reside. We note that clinics do not have to serve the entire state to be successful in NCVLI's mission to promote victims' rights. However, since it has also been acknowledged that it is a purpose of the clinics to represent individual victims in need, it follows that representation ought to be available to victims in all parts of a state.

One of the pieces of data that we asked the clinics to abstract for us was the counties in which 2007 cases originated. When we examined the distribution of cases by county, it immediately became clear that clinics varied considerably in terms of the geographic diversity of caseloads. As Figure 6.2 shows, cases of most of the clinics were concentrated in the counties where the clinics were based. The New Jersey clinic appeared to have the greatest diversity, with cases in all but two of the state's 21 counties and just 10 percent of its case load originating in the clinic's home county. In contrast, 53 of the Utah clinic's 85 cases originated in Salt Lake County, where the clinic is based. For the other clinics, between one-third and one-half of their case loads consisted of local cases.

Table 6.4 summarizes the preceding discussion of contrasts between the clinics on a number of the dimensions discussed in this section. Entries in the cells denote strong, moderate, or weak positions on each dimension.

Figure 6.2
Percentage of Cases in Clinics' Home Counties

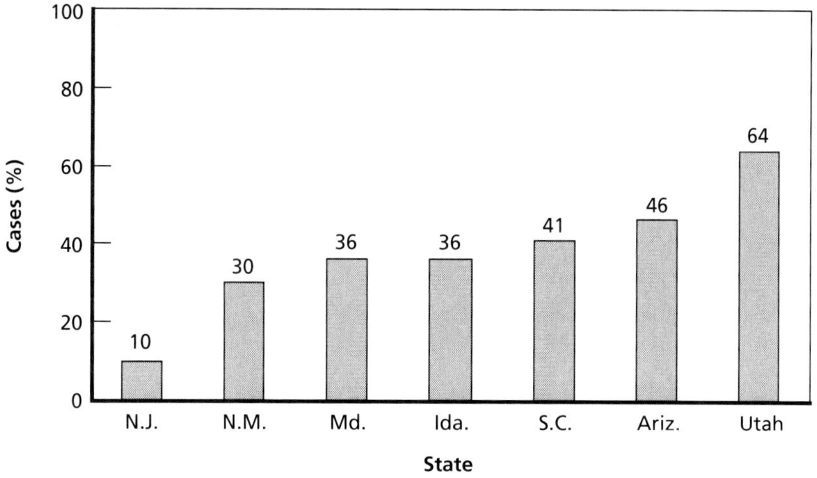

RAND *MG930-6.2*

Table 6.4
Comparison of Clinics on Key Process Measures

	Position						
Measure	Maryland	South Carolina	New Jersey	New Mexico	Idaho	Utah	Arizona
Relationship to victims' organization	Strong	Strong	Weak	Moderate	Weak	Moderate	Weak
Specialize in violence against women	Moderate	Strong	Moderate	Strong	Strong	Moderate	Weak
Holistic approach to client services	Strong	Strong	Strong	Weak	Weak	Moderate	Moderate
Community or victims' advocate as major source of referrals	Moderate	Strong	Strong	Moderate	Moderate	Strong	Moderate
Case load size	Moderate	Weak	Strong	Weak	Weak	Moderate	Weak
Geographic case load diversity	Moderate	Strong	Strong	Moderate	Moderate	Weak	Moderate

CHAPTER SEVEN

Clinic Work in Trial Courts

Trial-court advocacy is at the heart of the clinics' work on behalf of victims. Although the general outlines of this advocacy are the same in each clinic, there are some differences among them based both on the laws and legal culture of the states in which they operate and on the differing approaches of the clinic directors. In general, the clinics receive a call from a victim, conduct some type of intake screening, open a case, and then proceed—according to the victim's needs in the case—to do one or several of the following: contact the prosecutor, file a notice of appearance with the court, attend court proceedings to accompany the victim, raise oral arguments, file briefs and motions, and connect the victim with nonlegal services as needed.

Standing to Appear Before the Court

Although every state with a victims' rights legal clinic in this evaluation recognizes some form of victims' rights in its state constitution as well as state statutes, it is still unclear in several of those states whether victims have legal standing to assert their rights in court.[1] The argument could be made—and has been made, by NCVLI and some of the clinics—that victims' rights are meaningless without victim standing to assert them. However, some judges, prosecutors, and defense attorneys have been slow to accept the idea of victims and their attorneys

[1] A detailed discussion of the legal foundation for victim standing in each clinic state is included in Chapter Four.

being allowed to go before the judge and make oral arguments, file motions, or submit briefs. Where the statute or constitution does not explicitly spell out victim standing to assert their rights, and where challenges to standing have arisen, the clinics and advocates for victims have gone about trying to establish victim standing in different ways.[2]

Appealing a denial of standing to a higher court is one route to establish the right of victims and their attorneys to argue before a judge on matters affecting the victim's rights. However, clinics have had to tread carefully when considering appealing such denials, because losing an appeal of that nature would achieve the opposite of the desired outcome: It would establish legal precedent that victims do not have standing to seek enforcement of their rights in criminal court. We learned during our interview with staff from the New Jersey clinic, for example, about a case in which the victims were denied the right to be present at a waiver hearing and the judge refused to discuss the issue with the clinic director. Normally, in such a case, the clinic would ask the prosecutor to file an appeal to assert the victim's right to be present. However, in this case, the prosecutor declined to file the appeal, and so it was up to the clinic and the victims to decide whether to appeal. In this case, clinic staff reported, the victims and the clinic together decided not to appeal, because the clinic director feared not only losing the appeal on the clinic's right to be present but being challenged on the victim's standing to file the appeal in the first place, thereby creating bad law on standing.[3] Instead, the New Jersey clinic director has gone the route of working with state legislators to draft legislation that would revise the New Jersey victims' bill of rights to explicitly give victims standing to assert their rights. This legislation has passed the state assembly and is awaiting action in the state senate.

---

[2] Currently, victim standing is explicit only in Arizona's law and, to a more limited extent, Utah's and Maryland's. The South Carolina clinic has never been challenged on standing. The rest of the clinics have had to confront the issue in various ways.

[3] It is because of the lack of clarity in New Jersey law on victim standing that the clinic usually tries to have prosecutors file appeals on behalf of victims. The clinic director's reading of the current makeup of appellate-court judges causes him to fear that the appeals courts would reject an appeal from him based on lack of standing, and, should that happen, a victim's lack of standing to appeal would be enshrined in precedential case law.

The New Mexico clinic reports having mounted a successful appeal to a denial of standing. However, the decision was unpublished and therefore not technically binding precedential authority applicable to other cases. Despite the fact that it is not a formal opinion, the clinic lawyers have often successfully cited it as persuasive authority to establish standing when challenged.

In Maryland, victim standing was established through a series of appellate decisions as well as several statutory changes advocated by the clinic's parent organization, MCVRC. Once standing was established in law but not yet in practice, the clinic director provided assistance to a judge in drafting a rule to clarify the right of a victim's attorney to enter an appearance to represent the victim's rights. The rule was subsequently adopted, and the clinic cites it whenever it is challenged on standing. It has had no further problems entering appearances on behalf of victims.

Idaho is the clinic that has experienced the most serious setback when it comes to victim standing. After having accepted the clinic attorney's presence in court on a number of cases, a local judge sought explicit legal authority for the clinic's appearances in the courtroom. Finding none, he sent the clinic a letter asking it to justify its participation in criminal cases on behalf of victims. The clinic's response failed to persuade the judge, and he ordered his clerk to stop accepting filings from the clinic's attorney. Subsequently, another judge in a neighboring district followed the first judge's example and refused to accept the clinic's notices of appearance. The clinic is hoping that a new rule can be adopted to clarify the issue and get it back in those courtrooms where individual judges have denied them standing, despite the existence of victims' rights in the Idaho state constitution.

Clinics' Approach to Trial-Court Advocacy

Within the NCVLI legal-clinic project, there is an ongoing dialogue among NCVLI and the clinics about the system- and client-level goals of the clinics' legal work, as described in Chapter Two. NCVLI approaches the issue of victims' rights enforcement from a global system perspective and has the broad goal of changing the criminal-justice system and the legal culture so that victims' rights become as natural a part of the system, as defendants' rights are currently. The primary system-level goal of the clinic project is to create case law that fleshes out the victims' rights already in states' statutes and constitutions so that enforcement of those rights becomes commonplace. A second aspect of this movement to establish more-enforceable victims' rights law is to use the cases the clinics lose to demonstrate the need for better legislation, pass that legislation, and then, again, test it in court to establish precedential case law.[4] A third aspect of creating system change is to educate all actors in the criminal-justice system, but especially judges and prosecutors, so that victims' rights is no longer a novel concept but a natural part of the legal culture.

Broadly speaking, the legal clinics share these goals of NCVLI but also have client-focused goals that, at times, do not align with the larger system-level goals. Legal ethics bind the clinic attorneys to represent their clients' interests to the best of their abilities. This means that, if an individual victim seeks some action that will not further the system-change goals, the clinics must pursue it anyway. And conversely, if there is a victims' rights issue that the clinic believes it can use to establish good case law but the victim in that particular case is not interested, the clinic must forgo the action that could be beneficial to the movement as a whole. According to the clinic staff we interviewed, these differences arise in only a small number of cases. For the most part, what is good for individual victims is good for the movement. Also, from NCVLI's perspective, the system approach must always bow to the interests of the individual victim when the two do not align.

Another way in which these different emphases can be felt is in how the clinics prioritize the cases they accept. A more system-focused outlook would prioritize cases with the best potential for establishing case law favorable to victims' rights. This approach is generally followed by the Arizona clinic. A more client-focused outlook prioritizes helping as many victims as possible, whether or not a particular case

---

[4] Neither NCVLI nor the clinics use federal funds to lobby for legislation. They conduct all legislative advocacy either as individuals on their own time or using nonfederal funding.

has the potential for establishing legal precedent. This is the approach of the New Jersey clinic. But most of the clinics report taking all appropriate cases that are referred to them, which means that, by and large, the clinics are not turning away victims because their cases are not of interest to the victims' rights movement.

Sometimes, the clinics pursue an issue that does have the potential for establishing a written record, but the issue is resolved in such a way that it does not enter into the written record of the court, resulting in a win for the individual victim but no potential for influencing future cases. For example, the Maryland clinic represented a victim seeking funeral expenses through restitution. The judge inappropriately capped the amount of the restitution for this expense based on estate law, and, when the clinic filed an application for leave to appeal, the defense offered to pay the full amount the victim sought. Thus, the victim's goal was met without a need to appeal the trial court's decision to cap restitution. This was good for the victim in that case, but it also eliminated the possibility of establishing a precedent through appeal in favor of the general victims' right to full restitution.

The clinics, and many of the criminal-justice professionals and victims we interviewed, also believe that the mere presence of an attorney for the victim compels better behavior from all actors in the courtroom with regard to victims' rights. Again, this may be to the benefit of the current victim but without repercussions for future victims, if the behavior change is limited to those cases in which the attorney is physically present. Or it may suggest the need for victims' attorneys to always be present, just as defense attorneys are, to see that their clients' rights are enforced. The matter of short-term versus long-term behavior change in criminal-justice officials will be explored in the impact evaluation.

Another important difference among the clinics is the degree to which they practice informal advocacy on behalf of victims versus motion practice in court. Following on the preceding discussion, only motion practice (which creates a written record) can achieve the result of establishing new case law that advances the victims' rights legal movement. On the other hand, an individual client's problem may be more efficiently resolved with a call to the prosecutor that, if successful, spares the victim from having to spend time in court fighting for the right. Most clinics have found it beneficial, for their own ability to function, to try to work actively with prosecutors to ensure that victims get their rights and to file motions only when this approach is unsuccessful or insufficient. The one exception is the New Mexico clinic, which began with a more informal and cooperative approach toward prosecutors and has determined that more litigation is necessary to achieve success for its victims. The South Carolina clinic takes a different approach, spending much more time and energy on out-of-court work on behalf of victims than on motion practice in court.

Related to the emphasis on informal versus formal legal work is the question of when and how the clinics open a case and which services they provide to victims with and without a formal representation agreement. Arizona and New Jersey represent the two ends of the spectrum. In New Jersey, the clinic director will meet personally with any victim and make calls on the victim's behalf to the compensation board, the prosecutor, therapists, or other community resources, all without a formal representation agreement. According to the clinic director, if a victim comes in for a meeting and, afterward, there is further work to be done, then a case is opened and a representation agreement signed. With or without this agreement, the clinic makes every effort to connect victims to the resources they need, in many cases with a personal call from the clinic director to ensure that the connection is made. In Arizona, on the other hand, the clinic attorneys will not perform any informal advocacy on behalf of victims unless and until a representation agreement is signed. This is because Arizona legal ethics, in their view, dictate that either they represent a client or they do not and that, if they do not, then any informal advocacy is prohibited as unauthorized practice of law. If the Arizona clinic cannot represent a victim for whatever reason, it will refer the victim to another resource.

Victims' Rights Issues

Although the rights enumerated in each state's laws (constitution and statute) are somewhat different from state to state, the basic core of victims' rights is similar, and many of the same issues regularly come up for all of the clinics.

Precharge Cases

One issue with which the clinics have had to contend is whether to accept cases before charges are filed. For many victims, the initial complaint is that the investigation is not progressing or that the prosecutor is declining to file charges. Clinics have approached this issue differently. Some have sought meetings with the prosecutors and the victims to find out whether anything can be done to advance the case (or, alternatively, to help victims understand why the case cannot proceed if the clinic is in agreement with the prosecutor); New Jersey often takes this approach. In the first year of the Idaho clinic's operation, many of its cases were of this type, and the law students worked actively with police and prosecutors to try to push cases into prosecution. They had some success in getting cases that were still under investigation moved into prosecution but no success in changing prosecutors' previously made decisions not to proceed with a case. The Arizona clinic currently does not take state cases before charges being filed. It has found that precharge cases are time-consuming and technically are not victims' rights cases, since, under Arizona law, victims' rights do not attach until a case is filed in court. Under federal law, however, victims' rights attach upon the commission of the crime, so the Arizona clinic will take federal cases precharging.

Confer with the Prosecutor

Victims' right to confer with the prosecutor on plea agreements is an important area being addressed by all of the clinics. Many victims have turned to the clinics when they learned that prosecutors were accepting pleas to much lower offenses than those charged or with little to no jail time. In cases in which the victim is aware of the potential plea offer before it is submitted to the court, the clinic has an opportunity to intervene with the prosecutor and potentially offer arguments from the victim's perspective that cause the prosecutor to change aspects of the plea offer. Or, if the prosecutor is not willing to change the plea offer, victims can exercise their right to be heard and ask the judge not to accept the plea. In cases in which victims were not notified of the plea offer before it was submitted and accepted by the court, the clinics have sought redress of the violation of the victims' rights to be notified and heard, generally by asking that the plea be vacated and a new hearing held.[5]

Right to Privacy

Privacy of victim records, especially in sexual-assault cases, is a significant area of concern for many of the clinics. According to clinic directors, defense attorneys sometimes attempt to gain access to victims' confidential medical or counseling records through use of subpoenas during the discovery process or through challenges to restitution orders that include counseling expenses. The clinics and victims' advocates are concerned about the erosion of rape-shield protections when defense subpoenas for victims' records are allowed, and they fear that this may lead to fewer sexual-assault prosecutions. Prosecutors seem to share this concern, and several of the prosecutors we interviewed reported that having the clinics represent the victim's interest in these privacy cases has been very helpful. Judges appreciate hearing from both the state and the victim on these issues, according to both prosecutors and judges we interviewed. Challenges to defense subpoenas of victims' records are generally premised on the victims' right to privacy, dignity, respect, or to be free from harassment, as well as the states' specific rape-shield laws.

Right to Be Heard

Although victims' impact statements at sentencing are now fairly common in most jurisdictions, the clinics continue to litigate some issues involving the victim's right to be heard. These often involve the rights of more than one victim to be heard (for example, several survivors of a homicide victim) or the use of photos or audio or video recordings of the victim as part of the victim's impact statement. Some of the clinics have also litigated cases challenging the prohibition on sentencing recommendations from victims in death-penalty cases. The

---

[5] A New Jersey case of this type is discussed in Chapter Eight.

clinic cases on this issue have often involved a victim who wanted to advocate for a sentence other than death but was ordered to limit testimony to the impact of the crime and refrain from making any specific recommendations about the sentence. The clinics have also represented victims seeking to be heard on plea agreements, which is an area in which prosecutors in some jurisdictions continue to move quickly and neglect to hear from victims or inform them of the status of plea negotiations or even of hearings on plea agreements.

Right to Review the Presentence Report

In some states, victims have a right to view the presentence report. Presentence reports are important because the court frequently bases sentences on the recommendations contained therein, and errors may result in unjust sentences. This is obviously important for defendants, but it also matters for victims, as some of the information in those reports pertains to the victim and the impact of the crime. This is a newer area of victims' rights, and victims are granted the right to see these reports in only a few states (Arizona, Idaho, Colorado, and, to a limited extent, Utah). The federal CVRA does not include explicit permission for victims to have access to these reports, and the Arizona clinic argued unsuccessfully for such access in one federal case, *Kenna v. United States Dist. Court* (453 F.3d 1136, 9th Cir., 2006). In state court, the Arizona clinic generally does not have problems gaining access to presentence reports. In Idaho, victims are granted access to presentence reports; however, courts have been slower to allow access to victims' attorneys. The Idaho clinic has had both successes and failures at gaining access for its attorney and the victim to the presentence report.

Other Types of Assistance

The clinics also offer some assistance to victims in venues other than trial or appellate court. The New Mexico clinic fought for a victim's right to be present at parole hearings. It threatened to litigate but, in the end, did not have to. The parole board changed its procedures and now routinely allows victims to be present at parole hearings.

The clinics often will continue to help victims seek enforcement of restitution orders, even after these have been converted to civil orders. The Arizona clinic routinely files liens on behalf of victims with the Department of Motor Vehicles, the secretary of state, and the recorder of deeds, in order to capture restitution when an offender attempts to sell a car, boat, house, or other property.

Federal Cases

In the time since this evaluation was first funded, all of the clinics have expanded the scope of their work to include federal cases. However, for purposes of this evaluation, only federal work being done by the Arizona clinic was included, as that was the only clinic doing federal work when NIJ solicited proposals for the evaluation.

Most of the victims represented by the Arizona clinic in federal court are in cases referred from tribal courts. The clinic has done outreach on several Indian reservations and is building a reputation there as a valued outside party: not the government and not the defense. As a result of its work in one particular case, referrals have sharply increased from one of the Apache reservations in Arizona. In tribal cases, the clinic will start with the victim in tribal court and help ease the transition when the case moves from tribal to federal court, which can be an extremely intimidating process for victims. They must go from the reservation (wherever in the state that may be) to Phoenix and from a system that is based in their own culture and community to a large federal system. The legal issues in these cases tend to be the same or similar to the issues that arise in other cases, with the addition at times of working to get the federal courts to recognize certain aspects of the native culture where appropriate. For example, in one case, the Arizona clinic helped a domestic-violence victim get restitution to cover the costs of a Navajo cleansing ceremony she sought to aid her healing from the severe beating she experienced.

CHAPTER EIGHT

Clinic Work at the Appellate Level

When the clinics are successful at the trial level, there is no opportunity to bring cases up on appeal and establish precedential case law. In this way, appellate practice is often a judgment call related to service to the individual victim: The clinic must decide whether to push an issue that it is likely to lose *so that* it can appeal or whether it should not push the issue to spare the victim going through the appellate process, especially where the potential benefit to that particular victim may be minimal. Conversely, there may be issues that specific victims want to press on appeal, but the clinic must weigh the possibility of losing the appeal and creating bad law. In considering taking a victims' rights case up on appeal, it is important to have a victim who understands the risks of both filing and not filing an appeal and can make an informed decision. Defense-initiated appeals, on the other hand, do not present the same issues: If the defense appeals a victim's assertion of his or her right and the court accepts the case, the victim's side must be argued. When a clinic does not represent the victim, it still can provide the court with arguments based on victims' rights laws by filing amicus curiae (friend of the court) briefs.

When the clinic loses an appeal, this can help demonstrate the need for new legislation. The advocacy partners of the clinics often then take up those causes and win the passage of new legislation remedying the need discovered through the lost appellate case. The NCVLI clinics have had both wins and losses and have filed numerous amicus briefs as well, in state appellate and supreme courts. The signature wins have come on the issues of victim standing, the right to be heard, and the right to privacy. The losses relate primarily to the lack of remedies in the law for violations of victims' rights. Such losses play an important role in highlighting the need for new legislation to ensure the enforceability of crime victims' rights.

Clinic Cases Representing Victims

The Maryland clinic has had three appellate cases related to victim standing. In the first, *Surland v. State* (392 Md. 17, Md. Ct. App., 2006), the clinic represented the parents of a murder victim. The defendant was convicted and immediately filed an appeal. The defendant then died while the appeal was pending, and the defense attorney moved to have the court dismiss the appeal and vacate the conviction. Both the state and the victims opposed the defense motion to dismiss the conviction, with the clinic arguing that such a dismissal constituted unfair treatment of the victims, a violation of their rights under the law. When the defense attorney filed a petition with the state's highest court, the victims (through the clinic) filed a petition of their own, and the court of appeals ruled that the victims were not a party to the case and did not have standing to file petitions with the court. The case was therefore a loss on victim standing; however, it can be seen as contributing to the further evolution of victim standing in Maryland by illuminating the need for clearer rules and legislation with regard to standing. On the issue of unfair treatment, ultimately, the victims did get what they wanted: The defense was given 60 days for the deceased defendant's estate to appoint a substitute for the defendant so that the appeal could continue; when no substitute was appointed, the murder conviction was left intact.

In the second case related to victim standing, *Lamb v. Kontgias* (169 Md. App. 466, 2006), a registered victim of child sexual abuse was not notified of a hearing to reconsider her assailant's sentence. The question was whether the victim had standing to challenge a judgment vacating the original conviction and sentence. The Maryland Court of Special Appeals (Maryland's intermediate court of appeal) held that the circuit court had jurisdiction to decide whether the victim had standing to challenge the revised judgment. However, the court also determined that the victim could not challenge the sentence. The court held that any available remedy depended on legislative expansion of the victim's right to appeal.

The Maryland courts further clarified the issues of victim standing and remedies for violations of rights in the case of *Hoile v. State* (404 Md. 591, 2008). In that case, the clinic represented a victim who was not notified of hearings reconsidering the sentence of her assailant and, thus, was denied an opportunity to be heard at those hearings. The clinic, on behalf of the victim, sought to vacate the altered sentence on the grounds that she had been denied her rights. The trial court granted her request, and the defendant appealed.

The court found, significantly, that, under the newly expanded court rule, Maryland Rule 8-111, the victim had the right to participate in a criminal appeal in the same manner as a party regarding issues that directly and substantially affect the victim's rights. Clinic staff, therefore, was authorized to represent the victim in this case, including by participating in oral argument and filing a brief in the case.

However, the court in *Hoile* went on to find that the victim was not entitled to relief in the case. The legislature had not permitted a victim to seek invalidation of an otherwise legal sentence merely because the victim's rights concerning imposition of that sentence had been violated. The court noted, "Although a victim now has more opportunity to participate in an appeal, there remains no effective tangible remedy for a victim to seek to 'un-do' what already has been done in a criminal case." Thus, the *Hoile* case was a win on standing and a loss on remedies for victims' rights violations.

In a fourth case litigated by the Maryland clinic, *Lopez-Sanchez v. State* (388 Md. 214, Md. Ct. App., 2005), the court of appeals examined the question of whether a victim of a crime committed by a juvenile offender was entitled to seek reconsideration of a consent order for restitution that the trial court had approved without affording the victim his rights to notification or the opportunity to be heard. The court found that the right to seek a special appeal for a denial of victims' rights under section 11-103 of the criminal-procedure article did not extend to victims of delinquent acts and that, because the victim is not a party to a delinquency proceeding, a victim cannot exercise a general right to appeal.

The *Lopez-Sanchez* case is perhaps the best example of a clinic's loss at the appellate level leading directly to legislative change. A member of the clinic's pro bono panel that had represented the victim in *Lopez-Sanchez* successfully ran for state delegate during the period of representation. As a delegate, and following his loss in the courts, he cosponsored legislation to establish that victims' rights to appeal a denial of their rights also applies to victims of juvenile offenders. The legislation passed in 2006.

The New Mexico clinic had one successful appellate case in 2006 on victim standing, and, although it resulted only in an unpublished opinion, the clinic has been successful in citing it as persuasive authority in other cases. In that case, *Nasci v. Pope* (No. 29878, N.M., 2006), the clinic had represented a sexual-assault victim who sought to file a motion with the district court to attend all public court proceedings that the offender has a right to attend. After oral argument by the clinic attorneys, the state supreme court issued an order of remand granting the victim standing to assert her rights and ordering the district court to try to maximize the constitutional protections available to the victim under the state's statutes and constitution and the rules of procedure and evidence.

The Utah clinic has one appellate case pending at the time of this research (*State v. Lane*, Nos. 20070878, 20061126, S.C. Utah, oral argument September 3, 2008), in which it is representing two widows whose husbands were killed in a drunk-driving crash (the widows were injured in the crash). The victims allege that the prosecutor deliberately misled them about her planned plea agreement with the offender and then gave them the wrong hearing date so that they would not be there to object. Contrary to what the victims had initially been told by the prosecutor, the deal included no conviction if the offender complied with the conditions of the plea and limited restitution to $1,500, which the prosecutor then converted to a court fee, leaving the victims with nothing. The clinic seeks to have the court set aside the plea agreement on grounds that the victims' rights to notice, to be heard, and to be treated with fairness, dignity, and respect were violated and that the prosecutor committed a fraud upon the court when she asserted that the victims had been informed of the plea agreement and agreed with it.

The New Jersey clinic was also involved in an appellate case involving the failure to properly notify a victim of a plea agreement. In *State v. Means* (191 N.J. 610, 2007), the New Jersey Supreme Court considered the question of whether a trial court could set aside a plea agreement solely because the prosecutor failed to notify the victims before entering a plea agreement. In the case, a child abduction and molestation, the trial court accepted a plea without notifying the victim's parent as required under the state's victims' rights laws. The law center filed a motion to vacate the plea, and the motion was granted. The defense appealed, and the law center filed an amicus brief in the resulting state supreme-court case opposing the defendant's request to have the original plea bargain enforced. The state supreme court ruled that the failure to notify the victim was insufficient grounds to vacate a plea agreement. In its ruling, the court explained that, while a trial court should consider the victims' concerns, it may not impinge on a defendant's constitutional rights. The ruling noted that the trial court had vacated the guilty plea without having information to fairly evaluate the victim's concerns, because it did not know whether the victims had an objection to the plea agreement. Instead, the ruling continued, the trial court could have heard from the victims at sentencing, at which time it would have been in a better position to decide whether to continue to accept the terms of the plea agreement or to reject the plea. The matter was remanded to the trial court.

In an important Arizona privacy case, *P.M. v. Gould* (212 Ariz. 541, Ariz. Ct. App., 2006), the clinic represented a victim with cerebral palsy and developmental delays who had been molested by her father. When the state informed the court of its intention to call the victim's counselor as a witness to prove the aggravating factor of emotional harm, the defense subpoenaed the victim's counseling records, arguing that it needed the records to prepare for cross-examination of the counselor. The state agreed that the defense could have the records, and the trial court ordered an in camera review of these records. The clinic appealed with a special action to the Arizona Court of Appeals.

That appellate court found that the trial court should first determine whether the victim's counseling records or the counselor's testimony were essential to the state's effort to seek an aggravated sentence. The appellate court further declared that the trial court should balance the victim's constitutional right to refuse discovery against the state's interest in calling the counselor, especially in light of the fact that the state intended to prove six aggravating factors to the crime and only one was needed for the aggravated sentence. Furthermore, the appellate court indicated that, if the trial court still considered compelling the state's interest in calling the counselor to prove emotional harm, it should consider whether the counseling records were really necessary to cross-examine the counselor.

The clinics are not always successful in their appeals. For example, the Arizona clinic was especially disappointed in *State v. Glassel* (211 Ariz. 33, 2005), in which the Arizona Supreme Court rejected the argument that the victim had a right to inform the jury that he would prefer the defendant to be sentenced to life in prison rather than death. In this case, the victim was the widower of a homicide victim—his wife had been shot at a homeowner's association meeting by a disgruntled resident. The couple was two months short of their 50th wedding anniversary. The surviving victim had been in law enforcement his entire life and was aware that, if the defendant were sentenced to death, the case would not be over in his lifetime. Therefore, he wanted to ask for a sentence of life in prison during his victim's impact statement, but he was not allowed by the court to make a specific sentencing recommendation. Nationwide courts are split on this issue, and the clinic staff is hopeful that the issue will be resolved by the U.S. Supreme Court.

At the federal level, the Arizona clinic has had one big win and two losses. The win and one of the losses were both tied to the same case, that of Moshe and Zvi Leichner, a father and son, who defrauded numerous victims out of nearly $100 million. Kenna was one of their victims. In *Kenna v. United States Dist. Court* (435 F.3d 1011, 9th Cir., 2006), the clinic won Kenna the right to be heard at the sentencing of the second defendant, after the judge had refused to allow the same victims that had spoken at the sentencing of the first defendant to speak again. Kenna filed a petition for writ of mandamus with the ninth circuit, and the court concluded that, under the CVRA, "[v]ictims now have an indefeasible right to speak, similar to that of the defendant," and found that Kenna's statutory right was violated when the district court denied him the right to speak at Zvi Leichner's sentencing.

Kenna's second attempt to assert a victim's right—to read the presentence report—was not successful, however. Although this right is explicitly accorded to victims in some states, including Arizona, it is not spelled out in the CVRA, and, therefore, the clinic's seeking this right for Kenna in the federal case was a bit of a long shot. In that case, *Kenna v. United States Dist. Court* (453 F.3d 1136, 9th Cir., 2006), Kenna petitioned for a writ of mandamus to order the district court to release the presentence report to the victims. The U.S. Court of Appeals for the Ninth Circuit denied the petition, holding that the U.S. District Court for the Central District of California did not abuse its discretion or commit legal error when it found that the CVRA does not confer a general right for crime victims to obtain disclosure of a defendant's presentence report.

The Arizona clinic also received special permission to represent some victims in the Enron-related proceedings, which was in the fifth federal circuit (the clinic normally practices in the ninth circuit). Because the defendant, Kenneth Lay, died during the pendency of his federal direct appeal, restitution orders were voided. The clinic argued in *United States v. Lay* (456 F. Supp. 2d 869, S.D. Tex, *mand. denied*, 5th Cir., 2006) (unsuccessfully) that the victims should receive restitution from his estate despite his death.

The Idaho, Colorado, and South Carolina clinics have not yet taken any cases up on appeal.

Clinic as Amicus

When not directly representing the victim, the clinics will, at times, file amicus curiae briefs on victim-related issues before the appellate courts. According to the New Jersey clinic director, it is sometimes preferable to participate in a case as amicus, because doing so provides the opportunity to lay out all the relevant legal issues in an extensive brief, something that might not be appropriate in the context of representing the specific victim's interests. Among the amicus briefs of which we are aware that were filed by these clinics, two were in cases won by the victim. The other briefs either were not mentioned in the court's ruling or are in cases that are still pending.

One case was an appellate win on victims' right to privacy in New Jersey. The case, *State vs. Gilchrist* (381 N.J. Super. 138, 2005), pitted a rape victim's right to privacy against the defendant's right to confront his accuser. During his prosecution for aggravated sexual assault, kidnapping, burglary, and criminal restraint, the defendant filed a discovery motion requesting that a photograph of the victim be taken and provided to him. The trial court granted the request over the objections of the prosecutor. The appellate court reversed, stating that any possible benefits to the defendant from a court-ordered photograph were speculative and were outweighed by the victim's "right to privacy; her right to be treated with fairness, compassion, and respect; her right to be free from intimidation; and the need to encourage crime victims to cooperate and participate in the criminal justice system." The law center got involved as amicus when the defense appealed the case to the state supreme court. However, the case never made it to oral argument, because the defendant withdrew his appeal as part of a plea deal. Thus, the appellate ruling in favor of the victim stood, which was significant because it pitted the right to privacy against the right to discovery.

The other successful victim case was *Opert v. Criminal Injuries Comp. Bd.* (403 Md. 587, Md. Ct. App., 2008), in which the Maryland clinic filed an amicus brief and helped the victim's attorney to write his reply brief. Although the court declined the clinic's brief, the clinic notes that many of the arguments made in its declined amicus brief were, in fact, asserted in the court's opinion. The case involved a motorcyclist, Opert, who had been injured in a crash on the Baltimore beltway when a pedestrian walked out onto the highway with or on a bicycle in violation of the law. The issue was whether Opert was a "crime victim" for purposes of victim compensation. Lower courts and the compensation board had ruled that he was not. The court of appeals found that he was. Though the language of the statute was ambiguous, after examining the legislative history, the court agreed that finding Opert a "victim" was more likely reflective of the legislative intent.

Several of the briefs in unsuccessful or pending cases revolve around evidentiary issues in child sexual-abuse cases, such as whether to admit evidence or accusations of other assaults and whether to admit statements made by the victim to a social worker, as well as the protection of victims' private records. The South Carolina clinic filed a brief in a 2004 case (*In re Michael H.*, 360 S.C. 540, S.C. 2004) arguing against a defense request for a psychiatric evaluation of a child sexual-abuse victim, but the state's supreme court found the examination proper. The dissent echoed many of the arguments in the clinic brief.

Despite not yet having taken any clients, the Colorado clinic has filed one amicus brief on behalf of a dating-violence victim who was being asked to provide explicit proof that the relationship was "intimate" in order to invoke a domestic-violence sentencing enhancer. The case is pending (*State v. Disher*, 2008 Colo. LEXIS 432, Colo., 2008).

The NCVLI victims' rights clinics are actively pursuing appellate actions when (1) victims are denied their rights at the trial level, (2) a victim desires to press his or her case forward, and (3) when the clinic sees an opportunity to advance victims' rights through appellate case law. Though not all clinics have yet filed appeals, all report waiting for "the right case" to take up on appeal—that is, a case that offers both an opportunity for clarifying or broadening a victim's right and a good chance of the victim winning.

CHAPTER NINE

Implementation Challenges

This chapter discusses some of the implementation challenges the clinics have faced in their first few years of federal funding and how they have worked to overcome them. Some of the challenges, such as initial resistance from prosecutors and funding limitations, have affected all of the clinics, while other challenges have been experienced by only a few of the clinics.

Resistance to Change

Perhaps the biggest implementation challenge for the clinics overall has been finding ways to break down the resistance of prosecutors, and some judges, to the idea of victims being represented by attorneys in court. Although, as detailed in Chapter Two, victims' rights legislation has been in existence for more than 30 years, the NCVLI legal clinics represent the first concerted effort for victims to enforce those rights in court. For the two-party U.S. criminal-justice system, the integration of attorneys for victims has presented a significant challenge to traditional thinking.

The degree of prosecutor and judicial resistance has varied in the different clinic sites. As a former prosecutor, the director of the Utah clinic has been able to ease her former colleagues into an understanding of how victims' attorneys can support and not undermine the prosecutorial role. The New Mexico clinic, on the other hand, reports opposition so strong from prosecutors that one sought to eliminate the clinic's funding, while another "threw" a case because of the clinic's involvement. All of the clinics have had to conduct ongoing education campaigns, introducing themselves and the clinic's work to prosecutors repeatedly and clarifying the role they seek in helping victims to enforce their rights. New Mexico reports that crimes against children have served as a "bridge issue," as everyone seems to recognize the legitimacy of a child victim being represented by an attorney. These cases can help pave the way for adult victims' attorneys to also be accepted in court. With the clinics (with the exception of Colorado) now in their fourth or fifth year of operation, most report that prosecutor distrust has eased significantly over time, if not evaporated altogether.

Staff Turnover or Inexperience

Attorneys who are well suited to victims' rights work are not necessarily easy to find and keep, and this has proven to be another challenge for some of the clinics. There has been significant turnover of clinic leadership in South Carolina and Colorado (a clinic that has not yet taken any cases but is already on its third director). The Idaho clinic has transitioned from a supervising attorney who was a former judge, though not necessarily steeped in victims' rights, to a relatively inexperienced attorney whose background was in defendants' rights. There are various reasons for staff turnover, but the common thread for a number of the staff vacancies has been the uncertain funding stream. Attorneys who have families to support are apt to be lured by offers of more money and greater job security. According to NCVLI, an additional factor in attorney turnover may be vicarious trauma—attorneys may not have training in handling the emotional impact of working with crime victims day in and day out.

From what we found in our interviews with both clinic staff members and criminal-justice professionals, the turnover and lack of experience in these three clinics has impeded their progress to some degree. On the other hand, the clinics in New Jersey, Arizona, and Maryland are headed by three of the most prominent voices in the victims' rights movement nationally (the Arizona clinic's founder is not on staff, but the clinic is associated with his name regardless). The

Utah clinic also benefits from the distinguished victims' rights history of one of its board members. In these four clinics, the founders' and directors' long personal histories in victims' rights and strong personal reputations among criminal-justice professionals has clearly benefited the clinics, giving them access to a preexisting network of relationships statewide, including prosecutors and legislators. In New Mexico, the clinic director is a long-time and well-known victims' advocate, but there has been some attorney turnover; additionally, that clinic appears to have encountered even more resistance than other clinics among prosecutors to the idea of victims' attorneys.

In those clinics with less well-known attorneys and directors, outreach has proven to be somewhat of a challenge. Case loads in several of the clinics have been surprisingly low: just 17, 20, and 22 cases opened in 2007 in Idaho, New Mexico, and South Carolina, respectively. These clinics have to work harder both to get the word out about their availability for victims and to build confidence in their work among potential referral sources. All of the clinics with low case loads (based on the number of cases opened in 2007) report that their case loads are increasing as they become better known around the state and as criminal-justice system resistance to victims' attorneys lessens.

Demand for Services

Some clinics have had the opposite problem: more cases than they can comfortably handle. The Arizona clinic has recently implemented a waiting list, maxing out at about 40 cases (representing 55 to 60 victims) open at one time, while the New Jersey clinic may have as many as 100 cases open at any given time. The difference between these two clinics appears to be the amount of time spent in court: While the Arizona clinic attorneys attend every court proceeding with victims, the New Jersey attorneys attend court only when they expect a victims' rights issue to arise, and they instruct victims to call them if anything comes up when they are not there. The New Jersey clinic director also regularly works more than 80 hours per week. In Utah, the high demand for services led to their inability to screen cases quickly, which they believe led to a subsequent drop in referrals. However, they recently added a new attorney and believe that referrals will pick up again, as has happened in the past when word got around that their staff had increased.

Sustainability

Another significant implementation challenge for the clinics is securing funding. The federal funding under which the clinics currently operate has not always been secure from year to year, and nonfederal funding has been hard to come by. None of the clinics evaluated felt that it could survive without the federal grants, with the possible exception of Idaho, which is well integrated into the law school's clinical program. Several of the clinics did have additional sources of funding, most commonly state VOCA grants, and these funds allowed them to pay victims' advocates or outside contract attorneys for a certain number of hours (often less than full-time). When we asked the criminal-justice officials we interviewed about potential sources of funding for victims' attorneys, most felt that, to keep programs like the clinics going or to pay other attorneys representing victims, states would need to set aside a portion of offender fines (or levy new fines) for victims' legal services, or continued federal funds would have to be available for legal representation of victims.

As a way of controlling costs, NCVLI and the clinics initially envisioned making broad use of free help in the form of pro bono attorneys and law students. However, as the clinic implementation has progressed, NCVLI and most clinic directors have come to the conclusion that pro bono help is not as promising as was once thought, primarily because of a lack of the specialized knowledge that is required in victims' rights cases. Because it is a relatively new and complicated area of the law, a good deal of expertise is needed to be successful in many cases of the types taken by the clinics. Pro bono attorneys who specialize in other areas of the law require a good deal of training in victims' rights law. Law students have been helpful to some of the clinics with research, but their helpfulness is also bounded by their limited knowledge of the law and criminal procedure.

Clinic sustainability will be examined in more detail in the impact evaluation, through interviews with each clinic on its past, current, and projected future sources of funding, as well as other topics related to organizational sustainability.

CHAPTER TEN

Clinic Successes and Promising Practices

All of the clinics were able to point to numerous trial-court successes in ensuring that victims' rights were honored, and four of the seven active clinic sites had had at least one successful appellate case. Victims interviewed at each site sang the praises of the clinics and left no doubt that the clinics' work in individual cases was highly valued.

The different clinics had, mostly through trial and error and sometimes on instinct, developed certain practices that helped overcome challenges and led to specific successes. In this chapter, we highlight some of these promising practices.

Offering Help to Prosecutors

Several of the clinics were able to gain the good will of prosecutors by pointing out how their efforts could aid the prosecutors or save the prosecutors and their staff time. The most common ways that clinics make themselves helpful to prosecutors include the following:

- filing motions to protect the privacy of victim records. We were told several times in interviews with both prosecutors and judges that a clinic's asserting victims' privacy rights is more persuasive to judges than the prosecutor's argument alone.
- helping victims gather their paperwork on crime-related losses and calculate the amount of restitution to be requested. According to prosecutors interviewed, this saves an enormous amount of time for their victims' advocates. From the clinic perspective,

it also means that victims stand a better chance of receiving full restitution.
- at times, brokering the relationship with dissatisfied victims by helping them understand the legal system and why the prosecutor's office might be taking (or not taking) certain actions.

Offering Free Continuing Legal Education Training for Pro Bono Attorneys

Several of the clinics had offered or planned to offer free training for pro bono attorneys, for which the attorneys could receive CLE credit. This is a practice that could potentially overcome some of the hurdles to involving pro bono attorneys with victims' rights cases: specifically, their lack of knowledge both of victims' rights and of criminal procedure and the apparent lack of interest and willingness to take cases of this type. Many clinics noted that law schools focus almost exclusively on defendants' rights and, therefore, most practicing attorneys know little about victims' rights and do not even realize that it is a potential area of practice or pro bono work.

Writing Detailed and Well-Researched Briefs on Victims' Rights Issues

The New Jersey clinic director told us, "You have to blow everyone out of the water with your brief." Because the clinic attorneys are generally the most knowledgeable parties in the courtroom on victims' rights legal issues, their briefs should reflect that expertise. According to the New Jersey clinic director, when faced with a detailed, well-researched, and well-documented brief, a defense attorney will often accede to the victim's attorney's request rather than attempt to write a response brief on legal issues with which he or she is unfamiliar. Judges also appreciate these briefs because they serve to update them on a new area of law, and prosecutors, even when they know victims' rights laws, generally do not have the time to author such briefs.

Being Willing to Take a Risk

When a victim is willing to go through the appellate process, following that process to the end can pay major dividends for future victims. The New Mexico clinic's success in establishing standing for victims the *Nasci v. Pope* case was a result of the courage of the victim and the clinic's willingness to go with her all the way to the state's supreme court.

Using Losses to Spur Change

NCVLI and several of the clinics noted that a courtroom loss can be a win for the movement, because it often provides a concrete example of why current victims' rights legislation is not working. Several of the clinics hold regular meetings with advocacy groups (either internal or external to their organizations) to communicate about "holes" in victims' rights laws that are revealed by the cases the clinics lose and to strategize about advocating for legislative fixes for these holes.

Positioning the Clinic as the Expert on Victims' Rights

One successful form of outreach for gaining referrals was the New Jersey clinic's email list, through which it sends case updates and information on victims' rights to a wide array of criminal-justice practitioners and interested parties throughout the state. It also publishes a magazine once per year that provides in-depth analysis of important victims' rights cases and issues. These informational resources are appreciated by prosecutors, who view the clinic as the statewide expert on victims' rights and are likely to call it for assistance and refer it cases when victims' rights issues arise.

Gaining Word-of-Mouth Referrals

In the words of the South Carolina clinic director, "Do a good job on every case, and more cases will come, and change will come." Several of the clinics noted how one case in a particular community or from a particular referral agency led to more referrals from that community or agency when it saw and appreciated what the clinic did. Cultivating community-based referral sources was a very important strategy for gaining more cases and increasing the clinics' reach.

Offering Services to Victims in High-Profile Cases

The Idaho clinic, the only clinic situated in a rural area, watches the local news for crime cases and seeks out referral to those victims by contacting other professionals who may be in touch with the victims and asking them to provide the victims with the clinic's information. According to the Idaho clinic attorney, this entrepreneurial spirit is essential in an area that is somewhat remote and has fairly low crime rates.

Thinking Outside the Box on Sustainability

While most, if not all, clinics had applied for other grants in addition to NCVLI funding to sustain their clinic work, some had also come up with more-innovative ways to stretch their grant dollars. Of particular note were the Arizona clinic's subsidized office space provided by a corporate donor and the New Jersey clinic's law-firm model, through which the clinic director's salary is covered by the NCVLI grant, and his two law-firm partners work on typical civil legal cases and donate a portion of their profits, as well as pro bono hours, to the work of the clinic. The clinic also refers victims to the civil practice when appropriate, with fees from those cases contributing to the law firm's revenues. The Colorado clinic is exploring possibilities for direct funding from the state's 13 judicial districts, each of which has public funds it can dedicate to criminal-justice programs.

CHAPTER ELEVEN

Conclusions and Recommendations

From the information we gathered during the course of the process evaluation, we believe that the state clinics are beginning to fulfill the intentions of their architects and funders. All of the clinics have pushed the envelope of victims' rights in their state courts. Some have won significant victories in gaining standing for victims and expanding the definition of particular rights. Others are enjoined in the battle. But all have raised awareness of victims' rights with prosecutors, judges, defense attorneys, and police officials.

How much the clinics have managed to alter the legal culture remains to be determined through the second, or impact, phase of this evaluation. Two significant parts of that effort will be to (1) determine how court officials' opinions and observance of victims' rights has changed and (2) assess the extent to which basic victims' rights, such as being informed of rights or receiving restitution, have increased since the clinics opened. We plan to asses the former issue through systematic surveys with judges, prosecutors, victims' advocates, and defense attorneys who deal with felony cases and the latter issue through examination of case files from before and after the clinics opened their doors.

One of the good things about how NCVLI has gone about setting up the state clinic program is that it has funded different clinic models, as defined by where the clinics are housed, the kinds of cases in which they tend to specialize, whether they use litigation as a first or last resort, and how much use they make of pro bono attorneys or student help. This diversity creates the ability to explore the kinds of outcomes achieved by different models, in terms of the numbers and types of clients served, getting favorable published opinions or changes to court rules, and changing court officials' observances of victims' rights. For example, it may be that a successful pro bono program is associated with a greater number of clients served, while a focus on litigation is associated with successes in obtaining favorable published opinions on victims' rights. Although the small number of clinics and model types make definitive statements about the impact of the model type on the clinic outcomes impossible, we will explore these factors in the impact evaluation and attempt to identify any correlations between model types and outcomes.

One thing that the process evaluation has made clear is that clinics that build on the networks and reputations of experienced clinic directors and boards have an easier time than clinics that have to start from scratch. Clinics with directors and boards that are well connected gain more referrals and have more success getting prosecutors and judges to accede to their desired outcomes, even without having to litigate. A good part of their success may also result from trust that the directors have built up with local officials in their years of victims' rights work. It will be instructive to see whether the clinics starting from scratch are able to make up ground over time and develop the same kinds of respect and relationships that the Maryland, New Jersey, and Arizona clinics enjoy as a result of their directors' contacts or that the Utah clinic enjoys as a result of contacts of board members.[1]

Thoughts on the Future of the Demonstration Project

To the extent that we can tell at this point, the clinics have made significant progress in gaining acceptance for victims' rights. For the most part, they have done this by focusing on a small number of cases that have the potential to set precedent that will strengthen and expand the definition of victims' rights. Thus, they have acted, as NCVLI

---

[1] Of course, one of the dangers of an organization built on the strength and reputation of a single individual is that the organization may collapse when the individual leaves. It is not clear that this presents an immediate danger, since the clinics are still new and the directors are relatively young and very dedicated to their work.

intended, to increase court officials' awareness of victims' rights and to create new interpretations of law.

It is certainly true, however, that the clinics serve only a tiny fraction of their states' victims whose rights are not honored. The clinic model was never intended to accommodate large numbers of cases, yet the clinics' experience has pointed out that many court officials still feel that victims' rights are only to be accommodated when it is convenient or when they coincide with the interests of the justice system. It seems to us that the clinics have a significant role to play in thinking about how a larger number of victims could have recourse to assistance with rights issues—at a cost that is politically feasible.

The victims' rights clinics currently play at least three somewhat distinct roles. Although the attorneys probably do not intentionally segment their work in this way, in our evaluation, we observed that the work could more or less be divided into three categories: (1) informal advocacy that does not involve litigation (e.g., serving as a bridge between the victim and the prosecutor when there are disagreements); (2) litigation of the more common victims' rights issues (e.g., the ability to give a victim's impact statement or receive an order for full restitution); and (3) litigation of more-complex cases, including those that go up on appeal and have the potential for establishing appellate case law.

It strikes us that, perhaps, these three roles could actually be played by different groups of professionals to increase efficiency and reduce costs. The first role, that of intervening with prosecutors or other actors in the criminal-justice system in ways that outside of litigation, could be played by state compliance officers, who already work in some states and do this to a limited extent. The second role, that of litigating the more-common rights violations, could potentially be played by pro bono attorneys who have completed required training and with TA from an organization, such as NCVLI. The final role, that of litigating the more-complex and cutting-edge victims' rights cases, could be played by the more-experienced paid victims' rights attorneys at the NCVLI clinics. A limited expansion of this cadre to cover each state with at least one or two paid, experienced victims' rights litigators might do the job.

This model presents significant challenges. For example, the way in which most state compliance officers currently operate would not be sufficient to fill the role of what we are calling *informal advocacy*, because compliance officers' work most often happens after the fact and is geared more toward changing the system for future victims than for righting a wrong to a particular victim. For such professionals to be effective in current, ongoing cases, their mandate would need to be modified and prosecutors would have to be legally required to inform victims of the existence of such professionals so that victims could call on them in a timely manner. Victims' advocates would have to be trained and encouraged to alert compliance officers to potential problems at a point at which action can be effective and not after a plea has been taken or a sentence issued. Even so, many of the actions brought by a compliance officer would be too late to help a particular victim and would involve trying to change a pattern of rights violations emanating from particular counties or particular courtrooms.

The other weakness of using compliance officers for informal advocacy is that such advocacy by nonattorneys may not carry the same weight as informal advocacy by attorneys who have the ability to eventually litigate if the informal route proves unproductive. Therefore, such a compliance scheme would have to be designed with some sort of "teeth" that would provide a source of reserve power to the compliance officer comparable to that which attorneys possess by virtue of their ability to go before a judge.

There is also some risk in separating what we are calling *common* victims' rights issues from *complex* victims' rights issues. At the start of a case, it may not be apparent into which category a case may fall: A case that looks routine at the beginning may run into complexities that would entail the need to call in more-experienced litigators. Such transitions from one attorney to another might be upsetting and disruptive for victims and make for less-effective legal work than if the same attorney or team of attorneys stuck with a case from beginning to end. This possibility would have to be balanced against the potential benefit of having many more victims represented under this scheme.

Notwithstanding the limitations outlined here, the three-role concept represents a potential way to expand protections to a larger number of victims. There are surely other schemes that could be developed, and the impact phase of this evaluation may point the way to even more-effective practices for achieving more-consistent enforcement of victims' rights laws and helping more victims.

Thoughts on Future Evaluation Work

One thing that we noticed during the course of the process evaluation is that the clinics varied in the sophistication of their recordkeeping systems. The emphasis of the clinics is, appropriately, on serving clients and maintaining confidentiality of client information. We note, though, that in order for NCVLI and outside evaluators to be able to assess the work of the clinics, comprehensive and consistent recordkeeping is important.

We recommended—and the clinics agreed—to collect data on client demographics, essential to understanding the client base that the clinics serve. We also noted that the clinics have different ways of recording the presenting problems that bring clients to the clinics and the type of service that the clinics provide. Comparison of clinics would be facilitated if this information were recorded consistently from one clinic to the next. Developing consistent coding would entail NCVLI developing categories for recording data on these two dimensions and definitions of what those categories include. This would allow, for example, comparing the kinds of legal needs of families of homicide victims to the needs of sexual-assault victims.

Formal tracking and reporting of requests for clinic services and clients turned away or wait-listed would also help NCVLI to evaluate staffing levels of the clinics and make the argument that more staff were needed in particular states. It would also be useful if the clinics tracked and reported the number of attorney hours spent on gathering information from potential clients, conferencing with clients, advocating for clients' legal needs, spending time in court, and connecting clients with needed social services. That would allow NCVLI and others interested in measuring clinic performance to compare NCVLI's statistics to public service standards for reasonable caseloads per attorney and determine how efficiently clinics are serving their clients.

Lastly, the client-satisfaction surveys should be expanded and reported with greater regularity. Client satisfaction is an important yardstick to gauge how the clinics are doing. Surveys are done now, but they are few in number and not reported on a consistent basis. NCVLI should insist that clinics forward satisfaction surveys for all cases that are opened by the clinics (or a written record of unsuccessful attempts to conduct the interviews). NCVLI should also consider contracting this function out, in order to reduce bias that is likely to occur when the same individual who provides service to victims also queries them about their satisfaction with those services.

Final Thoughts

This process evaluation has begun to shine a light on the work being done in eight state clinics on very limited budgets; more remains to be seen about the effectiveness of this work and the best ways to obtain for all crime victims the rights, respect, and dignity for which countless advocates have long struggled.

References

Alabama Code, Title 15, Criminal Procedure, Chapter 23, Alabama Crime Victims, Section 83, Assertion of Rights by Attorney General or District Attorney.

Albuquerque Rape Crisis Ctr. v. Blackmer, 138 N.M. 398, 120 P.3d 820, August 18, 2005.

Arizona Administrative Code, Title 9, Health Services, Article 11, STD-Related Testing and Notification, Section R9-6-1104, Court-Ordered STD-Related Testing. As of September 11, 2009: http://www.azsos.gov/public_services/Title_09/9-06.htm#ARTICLE_11

Arizona Constitution, Article II, Bill of Rights, Section 2.1, Victims' Bill of Rights.

Arizona Revised Statutes, Title 8, Children, Chapter 3, Juvenile Offenders, Article 3, Disposition and Commitment, Section 344, Restitution Payments. As of September 11, 2009: http://www.azleg.state.az.us/FormatDocument.asp?inDoc=/ars/8/00344.htm&Title=8&DocType=ARS

———, Title 8, Children, Chapter 3, Juvenile Offenders, Article 7, Victims' Rights for Juvenile Offenses, Section 390, Notice of Proceedings. As of September 11, 2009: http://www.azleg.state.az.us/FormatDocument.asp?inDoc=/ars/8/00390.htm&Title=8&DocType=ARS

———, Title 8, Children, Chapter 3, Juvenile Offenders, Article 7, Victims' Rights for Juvenile Offenses, Section 418, Implementation Fee, Definition. As of September 11, 2009: http://www.azleg.state.az.us/FormatDocument.asp?inDoc=/ars/8/00418.htm&Title=8&DocType=ARS

———, Title 8, Children, Chapter 3, Juvenile Offenders, Article 7, Victims' Rights for Juvenile Offenses, Section 382, Definitions. As of September 11, 2009: http://www.azleg.state.az.us/FormatDocument.asp?inDoc=/ars/8/00382.htm&Title=8&DocType=ARS

———, Title 8, Children, Chapter 3, Juvenile Offenders, Article 7, Victims' Rights for Juvenile Offenses, Section 383.01, Victims' Rights, Dismissed Counts. As of September 14, 2009:
http://www.azleg.state.az.us/FormatDocument.asp?inDoc=/ars/8/00383-01.htm&Title=8&DocType=ARS

———, Title 8, Children, Chapter 3, Juvenile Offenders, Article 7, Victims' Rights for Juvenile Offenses, Section 385.01, Victims' Rights for Neighborhood Associations. As of September 11, 2009:
http://www.azleg.state.az.us/FormatDocument.asp?inDoc=/ars/8/00385-01.htm&Title=8&DocType=ARS

———, Title 8, Children, Chapter 3, Juvenile Offenders, Article 7, Victims' Rights for Juvenile Offenses, Section 396, Notice of Probation Modification, Termination or Revocation Disposition Matters, Notice of Arrest. As of September 14, 2009:
http://www.azleg.state.az.us/FormatDocument.asp?inDoc=/ars/8/00396.htm&Title=8&DocType=ARS

———, Title 8, Children, Chapter 3, Juvenile Offenders, Article 7, Victims' Rights for Juvenile Offenses, Section 412, Victim's Right to Refuse an Interview, Applicability. As of September 11, 2009:
http://www.azleg.state.az.us/FormatDocument.asp?inDoc=/ars/8/00412.htm&Title=8&DocType=ARS

———, Title 8, Children, Chapter 3, Juvenile Offenders, Article 7, Victims' Rights for Juvenile Offenses, Section 421, Statement of Rights. As of September 11, 2009:
http://www.azleg.state.az.us/FormatDocument.asp?inDoc=/ars/8/00421.htm&Title=8&DocType=ARS

———, Title 8, Children, Chapter 3, Juvenile Offenders, Article 7, Victims' Rights for Juvenile Offenses, Section 416, Standing to Invoke Rights, Recovery of Damages, Right to Counsel. As of September 11, 2009:
http://www.azleg.state.az.us/FormatDocument.asp?inDoc=/ars/8/00416.htm&Title=8&DocType=ARS

———, Title 11, Counties, Chapter 3, County Officers, Article 3, Recorder, Section 483, Records Maintained by County Recorder, Confidentiality, Definitions. As of September 11, 2009:
http://www.azleg.state.az.us/FormatDocument.asp?inDoc=/ars/11/00483.htm&Title=11&DocType=ARS

———, Title 11, Counties, Chapter 3, County Officers, Article 3, Recorder, Section 484, Records Maintained by County Assessor and County Treasurer, Redaction, Definition. As of September 11, 2009:
http://www.azleg.state.az.us/FormatDocument.asp?inDoc=/ars/11/00484.htm&Title=11&DocType=ARS

———, Title 12, Courts and Civil Proceedings, Chapter 6, Special Actions and Proceedings by Individual Persons, Article 1, Change of Name, Section 601, Application, Venue, Judgment. As of September 11, 2009: http://www.azleg.state.az.us/FormatDocument.asp?inDoc=/ars/12/00601.htm&Title=12&DocType=ARS

———, Title 12, Courts and Civil Proceedings, Chapter 6, Special Actions and Proceedings by Individual Persons, Article 12, Miscellaneous, Section 716, Injury During Criminal Acts, Civil Actions, Presumptions, Definition. As of September 11, 2009: http://www.azleg.state.az.us/FormatDocument.asp?inDoc=/ars/12/00716.htm&Title=12&DocType=ARS

———, Title 13, Criminal Code, Chapter 1, General Provisions, Section 101.01, Additional Purposes of the Criminal Law. As of September 11, 2009: http://www.azleg.state.az.us/FormatDocument.asp?inDoc=/ars/13/00101-01.htm&Title=13&DocType=ARS

———, Title 13, Criminal Code, Chapter 7, Imprisonment, Section 701, Sentence of Imprisonment for Felony, Presentence Report, Aggravating and Mitigating Factors, Consecutive Terms of Imprisonment, Definition. As of September 11, 2009: http://www.azleg.state.az.us/FormatDocument.asp?inDoc=/ars/13/00701.htm&Title=13&DocType=ARS

———, Title 13, Criminal Code, Chapter 7, Imprisonment, Section 703, Repetitive Offenders, Sentencing. As of September 11, 2009: http://www.azleg.state.az.us/FormatDocument.asp?inDoc=/ars/13/00703.htm&Title=13&DocType=ARS

———, Title 13, Criminal Code, Chapter 7, Imprisonment, Section 703.01.

———, Title 13, Criminal Code, Chapter 8, Restitution and Fines, Section 805, Jurisdiction. As of September 11, 2009: http://www.azleg.state.az.us/FormatDocument.asp?inDoc=/ars/13/00805.htm&Title=13&DocType=ARS

———, Title 13, Criminal Code, Chapter 8, Restitution and Fines, Section 810, Consequences of Nonpayment of Fines, Fees, Restitution or Incarceration Costs. As of September 11, 2009: http://www.azleg.state.az.us/FormatDocument.asp?inDoc=/ars/13/00810.htm&Title=13&DocType=ARS

———, Title 13, Criminal Code, Chapter 9, Probation and Restoration of Civil Rights, Section 902, Periods of Probation, Monitoring, Fees. As of September 11, 2009: http://www.azleg.state.az.us/FormatDocument.asp?inDoc=/ars/13/00902.htm&Title=13&DocType=ARS

———, Title 13, Criminal Code, Chapter 9, Probation and Restoration of Civil Rights, Section 923, Persons Convicted of Sexual Offenses, Annual Probation Review Hearing, Report, Notification. As of September 11, 2009: http://www.azleg.state.az.us/FormatDocument.asp?inDoc=/ars/13/00923.htm&Title=13&DocType=ARS

———, Title 13, Criminal Code, Chapter 13, Kidnapping and Related Offenses, Section 1309, Restitution. As of September 11, 2009: http://www.azleg.state.az.us/FormatDocument.asp?inDoc=/ars/13/01309.htm&Title=13&DocType=ARS

———, Title 13, Criminal Code, Chapter 38, Miscellaneous, Article 18, Appeals, Section 4042, Appellate Proceedings, Request for Extension, Victim Notification. As of September 11, 2009: http://www.azleg.state.az.us/FormatDocument.asp?inDoc=/ars/13/04042.htm&Title=13&DocType=ARS

———, Title 13, Criminal Code, Chapter 38, Miscellaneous, Article 21, Attendance of Witnesses, Section 4071, Subpoena, Issuance, Duty of Clerk. As of September 11, 2009: http://www.azleg.state.az.us/FormatDocument.asp?inDoc=/ars/13/04071.htm&Title=13&DocType=ARS

———, Title 13, Criminal Code, Chapter 38, Miscellaneous, Article 27, Crime Victim Accounts, Section 4202, Void Contracts, Crime Victim Accounts, Establishment, Notice to Vicims, Exceptions, Civil Liability, Definition. As of September 11, 2009: http://www.azleg.state.az.us/FormatDocument.asp?inDoc=/ars/13/04202.htm&Title=13&DocType=ARS

———, Title 13, Criminal Code, Chapter 38, Miscellaneous, Article 29, Post-Conviction Relief, Section 4234.01, Post-Conviction Relief Proceedings, Request for Extension, Victim Notification. As of September 11, 2009: http://www.azleg.state.az.us/FormatDocument.asp?inDoc=/ars/13/04234-01.htm&Title=13&DocType=ARS

———, Title 13, Criminal Code, Chapter 40, Crime Victims' Rights, Section 4401, Definitions. As of September 11, 2009: http://www.azleg.state.az.us/FormatDocument.asp?inDoc=/ars/13/04401.htm&Title=13&DocType=ARS

———, Title 13, Criminal Code, Chapter 40, Crime Victims' Rights, Section 4402.01, Victims' Rights, Dismissed Counts. As of September 11, 2009: http://www.azleg.state.az.us/FormatDocument.asp?inDoc=/ars/13/04402-01.htm&Title=13&DocType=ARS

———, Title 13, Criminal Code, Chapter 40, Crime Victims' Rights, Section 4405, Information Provided to Victim by Law Enforcement Agencies. As of September 11, 2009: http://www.azleg.state.az.us/FormatDocument.asp?inDoc=/ars/13/04405.htm&Title=13&DocType=ARS

———, Title 13, Criminal Code, Chapter 40, Crime Victims' Rights, Section 4409, Notice of Criminal Proceedings. As of September 11, 2009: http://www.azleg.state.az.us/FormatDocument.asp?inDoc=/ars/13/04409.htm&Title=13&DocType=ARS

———, Title 13, Criminal Code, Chapter 40, Crime Victims' Rights, Section 4411, Notice of Post-Conviction Review and Appellate Proceedings. As of September 11, 2009: http://www.azleg.state.az.us/FormatDocument.asp?inDoc=/ars/13/04411.htm&Title=13&DocType=ARS

———, Title 13, Criminal Code, Chapter 40, Crime Victims' Rights, Section 4415, Notice of Probation Modification, Termination or Revocation Disposition Matters, Notice of Arrest. As of September 11, 2009: http://www.azleg.state.az.us/FormatDocument.asp?inDoc=/ars/13/04415.htm&Title=13&DocType=ARS

———, Title 13, Criminal Code, Chapter 40, Crime Victims' Rights, Section 4426, Sentencing. As of September 11, 2009: http://www.azleg.state.az.us/FormatDocument.asp?inDoc=/ars/13/04426.htm&Title=13&DocType=ARS

———, Title 13, Criminal Code, Chapter 40, Crime Victims' Rights, Section 4426.01, Sentencing, Victims' Right to Be Heard. As of September 11, 2009: http://www.azleg.state.az.us/FormatDocument.asp?inDoc=/ars/13/04426-01.htm&Title=13&DocType=ARS

———, Title 13, Criminal Code, Chapter 40, Crime Victims' Rights, Section 4433, Victim's Right to Refuse an Interview, Applicability. As of September 11, 2009: http://www.azleg.state.az.us/FormatDocument.asp?inDoc=/ars/13/04433.htm&Title=13&DocType=ARS

———, Title 13, Criminal Code, Chapter 40, Crime Victims' Rights, Section 4434, Victim's Right to Privacy, Exception. As of September 11, 2009: http://www.azleg.state.az.us/FormatDocument.asp?inDoc=/ars/13/04434.htm&Title=13&DocType=ARS

———, Title 13, Criminal Code, Chapter 40, Crime Victims' Rights, Section 4435, Speedy Trial, Continuance, Notice. As of September 11, 2009: http://www.azleg.state.az.us/FormatDocument.asp?inDoc=/ars/13/04435.htm&Title=13&DocType=ARS

———, Title 13, Criminal Code, Chapter 40, Crime Victims' Rights, Section 4436, Effect of Failure to Comply. As of September 11, 2009: http://www.azleg.state.az.us/FormatDocument.asp?inDoc=/ars/13/04436.htm&Title=13&DocType=ARS

———, Title 13, Criminal Code, Chapter 40, Crime Victims' Rights, Section 4437, Standing to Invoke Rights, Recovery of Damages, Right to Counsel. As of September 11, 2009: http://www.azleg.state.az.us/FormatDocument.asp?inDoc=/ars/13/04437.htm&Title=13&DocType=ARS

———, Title 13, Criminal Code, Chapter 40, Crime Victims' Rights, Section 4438, Statement of Rights. As of September 11, 2009: http://www.azleg.state.az.us/FormatDocument.asp?inDoc=/ars/13/04438.htm&Title=13&DocType=ARS

———, Title 13, Criminal Code, Chapter 40, Crime Victims' Rights, Section 4439, Right to Leave Work, Scheduled Proceedings, Counseling, Employment Rights, Nondiscrimination, Confidentiality, Definition. As of September 11, 2009: http://www.azleg.state.az.us/FormatDocument.asp?inDoc=/ars/13/04439.htm&Title=13&DocType=ARS

———, Title 13, Criminal Code, Chapter 40, Crime Victims' Rights, Section 4440, Notice of Petition of Factual Innocence, Right to Be Heard, Hearing. As of September 11, 2009: http://www.azleg.state.az.us/FormatDocument.asp?inDoc=/ars/13/04440.htm&Title=13&DocType=ARS

———, Title 16, Elections and Electors, Chapter 1, Qualification and Registration of Electors, Article 4, Forms, Section 153, Voter Registration, Confidentiality, Definitions. As of September 11, 2009: http://www.azleg.state.az.us/FormatDocument.asp?inDoc=/ars/16/00153.htm&Title=16&DocType=ARS

———, Title 28, Transportation, Chapter 2, Administration, Article 5, Records, Section 455, Release of Personal Information, Fees. As of September 11, 2009: http://www.azleg.state.az.us/FormatDocument.asp?inDoc=/ars/28/00455.htm&Title=28&DocType=ARS

———, Title 28, Transportation, Chapter 2, Administration, Article 5, Records, Section 456, Subsequent Sale or Disclosure of Record Information by Authorized Recipient. As of September 11, 2009: http://www.azleg.state.az.us/FormatDocument.asp?inDoc=/ars/28/00456.htm&Title=28&DocType=ARS

———, Title 28, Transportation, Chapter 2, Administration, Article 5, Records, Section 457, Unlawful Acts, Classification, Civil Actions. As of September 11, 2009:
http://www.azleg.state.az.us/FormatDocument.asp?inDoc=/ars/28/00457.htm&Title=28&DocType=ARS

———, Title 28, Transportation, Chapter 2, Administration, Article 5, Records, Section 458, Motor Vehicle Records Release, Department Review Panel. As of September 11, 2009:
http://www.azleg.state.az.us/FormatDocument.asp?inDoc=/ars/28/00458.htm&Title=28&DocType=ARS

———, Title 28, Transportation, Chapter 3, Traffic and Vehicle Regulation, Article 4, Accidents, Section 672, Causing Serious Physical Injury or Death by a Moving Violation, Classification, Penalties. As of September 11, 2009:
http://www.azleg.state.az.us/FormatDocument.asp?inDoc=/ars/28/00672.htm&Title=28&DocType=ARS

———, Title 31, Prisons and Prisoners, Chapter 2, State Prison, Article 2, Prisoners, Section 230, Prisoner Spendable Accounts. As of September 11, 2009:
http://www.azleg.state.az.us/FormatDocument.asp?inDoc=/ars/31/00230.htm&Title=31&DocType=ARS

———, Title 31, Prisons and Prisoners, Chapter 2, State Prison, Article 3, Labor by Prisoners, Section 254, Compensation for Labor Performed, Price of Prison Made Articles, Distribution of Earnings, Workers' Compensation. As of September 11, 2009:
http://www.azleg.state.az.us/FormatDocument.asp?inDoc=/ars/31/00254.htm&Title=31&DocType=ARS

———, Title 31, Prisons and Prisoners, Chapter 2, State Prison, Article 4, Products of Prisoners, Section 261, Sale or Exchange of Products of Individual Prisoners. As of September 11, 2009:
http://www.azleg.state.az.us/FormatDocument.asp?inDoc=/ars/31/00261.htm&Title=31&DocType=ARS

———, Title 31, Prisons and Prisoners, Chapter 2, State Prison, Article 6, Transition Program, Section 281, Transition Program, Drug Offenders, Report. As of September 11, 2009:
http://www.azleg.state.az.us/FormatDocument.asp?inDoc=/ars/31/00281.htm&Title=31&DocType=ARS

———, Title 33, Property, Chapter 10, Arizona Residential Landlord and Tenant Act, Article 4, Remedies, Section 1361, Noncompliance by the Landlord. As of September 11, 2009:
http://www.azleg.state.az.us/FormatDocument.asp?inDoc=/ars/33/01361.htm&Title=33&DocType=ARS

———, Title 39, Public Records, Printing and Notices, Chapter 1, Public Records, Article 2, Searches and Copies, Section 123, Information Identifying Eligible Persons, Confidentiality, Definitions. As of September 11, 2009: http://www.azleg.state.az.us/FormatDocument.asp?inDoc=/ars/39/00123.htm&Title=39&DocType=ARS

———, Title 39, Public Records, Printing and Notices, Chapter 1, Public Records, Article 2, Searches and Copies, Section 124, Releasing Information Identfying an Eligible Person, Violations, Classification, Definitions. As of September 11, 2009:
http://www.azleg.state.az.us/FormatDocument.asp?inDoc=/ars/39/00124.htm&Title=39&DocType=ARS

———, Title 39, Public Records, Printing and Notices, Article 2, Searches and Copies, Section 127, Free Copies of Police Reports and Transcripts for Crime Victims, Definitions. As of September 11, 2009:
http://www.azleg.state.az.us/FormatDocument.asp?inDoc=/ars/39/00127.htm&Title=39&DocType=ARS

Arizona Rules of Criminal Procedure, Chapter II, Preliminary Proceedings, Rule 4, Initial Appearance and Arraignment, Rule 4.2, Initial Appearance.

———, Chapter IV, Pretrial Procedures, Rule 15, Disclosure, Rule 15.1, Disclosure by State.

———, Chapter IV, Pretrial Procedures, Rule 15, Disclosure, Rule 15.7, Sanctions.

———, Chapter VII, Postverdict Proceedings, Rule 26, Judgment, Presentence Report, Presentence Hearing, Sentence, Rule 26.12, Definitions, Scope.

———, Chapter VII, Postverdict Proceedings, Rule 27, Probation and Probation Revocation, Rule 27.2, Intercounty Transfers.

———, Chapter VII, Postverdict Proceedings, Rule 27, Probation and Probation Revocation, Rule 27.12, Probation Review Hearing.

———, Chapter VII, Postverdict Proceedings, Rule 27, Probation and Probation Revocation, Rule 27.11, Victims Rights in Probation Proceedings.

———, Chapter VIII, Appeal and Other Post-Conviction Relief, Rule 31, Appeal from Superior Court, Rule 31.27, Extensions of Time, Notification of Victim.

———, Chapter VIII, Appeal and Other Post-Conviction Relief, Rule 32, Other Post-Conviction Relief, Rule 32.10, Extensions of Time, Notification of Victims.

Cassell, Paul G., "Balancing the Scales of Justice: The Case for and the Effects of Utah's Victims' Rights Amendment," *Utah Law Review*, No. 4, 1994, pp. 1373–1469.

Chaney v. State, 397 Md. 460, 918 A.2d 506, March 14, 2007.

Colorado Constitution, Article II, Bill of Rights, Section 16a, Rights of Crime Victims.

Colorado Current Rule 1505-13, Address Confidentiality Program Rules. As of September 11, 2009: http://www.sos.state.co.us/pubs/rule_making/ACP_rules.pdf

Colorado Revised Statutes, Title 12, Professions and Occupations, Article 61, Real Estate, Part 9, Mortgage Brokers, Section 905.5, Disciplinary Actions: Grounds, Procedures, Rules.

———, Title 13, Courts and Court Procedure, Article 14, Civil Protection Orders, Section 102, Civil Protection Orders: Legislative Declaration.

———, Title 16, Criminal Proceedings, Article 3, Arrest: Searches and Seizures, Part 5, Warrants and Bonds for Persons Illegally in the Country, Section 502, No Dismissal of Cases Against Persons Illegally in the Country.

———, Title 17, Corrections, Article 1, Department of Corrections, Section 115.5, Prison Sexual Assault Prevention Program.

———, Title 18, Criminal Code, Article 3, Offenses Against the Person, Part 4, Unlawful Sexual Behavior, Section 407.5, Victim Evidence: Forensic Evidence: Electronic Lie Detector Exam Without Victim's Consent Prohibited.

———, Title 18, Criminal Code, Article 3, Offenses Against the Person, Part 4, Unlawful Sexual Behavior, Section 417, Reports of Sexual Assault by Applicants, Registrants, or Licensed Professionals.

———, Title 19, Children's Code, Article 2, The Colorado Juvenile Justice System, Part 2, Administrative Entities: Agents, Section 214, Detention Center Sexual Assault Prevention Program.

———, Title 19, Children's Code, Article 2, The Colorado Juvenile Justice System, Part 3, Juvenile Administrative Programs: Services, Section 303, Juvenile Diversion Program: Authorized.

———, Title 19, Children's Code, Article 2, The Colorado Juvenile Justice System, Part 7, Preadjudication, Section 708, Entry of Plea.

———, Title 19, Children's Code, Article 2, The Colorado Juvenile Justice System, Part 10, Postsentence, Section 1002, Juvenile Parole.

———, Title 24, Government: State, Article 4.1, Crime Victim Compensation and Victim and Witness Rights, Part 3, Guidelines for Assuring the Rights of Victims of and Witnesses to Crimes, Section 302.5, Rights Afforded to Victims.

———, Title 24, Government: State, Article 4.1, Crime Victim Compensation and Victim and Witness Rights, Part 3, Guidelines for Assuring the Rights of Victims of and Witnesses to Crimes, Section 303, Procedures for Assuring Rights of Victims of Crimes.

———, Title 24, Government: State, Article 21, Secretary of State: Department of State, Part 2, Address Confidentiality for Victims of Domestic Violence, a Sexual Offense, or Stalking.

———, Title 24, Government: State, Article 33.5, Public Safety, Part 4, Colorado Bureau of Investigation, Section 425, Cold Case Homicide Team.

———, Title 24, Government: State, Article 72, Public Records, Part 2, Inspection, Copying, or Photographing, Section 204, Allowance or Denial or Inspection: Grounds, Procedure, Appeal, Definitions.

———, Title 24, Government: State, Article 72, Public Records, Part 3, Criminal Justice Records, Section 306, Copies, Printouts, or Photographs of Criminal Justice Records: Fees Authorized.

———, Title 25, Health, Article 3, Hospitals, Section 110, Emergency Contraception: Definitions.

Connecticut General Statutes, Title 46a, Human Rights, Chapter 813a, Office of the Victim Advocate, Office of the Child Advocate, Section 13c, Responsibilities of the Victim Advocate. As of September 11, 2009:
http://www.cga.ct.gov/2009/pub/chap813a.htm#Sec46a-13c.htm

"Constitutionalizing Crime Victim Rights," *Criminal Law Bulletin*, Vol. 33, No. 5, 1997, pp. 395–423.

Coscarelli, Kate, "If Not for a Murdered Teen, Victims Would See Little Help," *Star-Ledger*, September 21, 2003, p. 15.

Davis, Robert C., James M. Anderson, Julie Whitman, and Susan Howley, *Securing Rights for Victims: A Process Evaluation of the National Crime Victim Law Institute's Victims' Rights Clinics*, Santa Monica, Calif.: RAND Corporation, MG-930-NIJ, 2009. As of December 2009:
http://www.rand.org/pubs/monographs/MG930/

DOJ—*see* U.S. Department of Justice.

Douglass v. State, 219 Ariz. 152, 195 P.3d 189, Ariz. Ct. App., April 10, 2008.

Felicioni v. Administrative Office of the Courts, 404 N.J. Super. 382, 961 A.2d 1207, December 15, 2008.

Florida Statutes, Title XLVII, Criminal Procedure and Corrections, Chapter 960, Victim Assistance, Section 1, Guidelines for Fair Treatment of Victims and Witnesses in the Criminal Justice and Juvenile Justice Systems. As of September 11, 2009:
http://www.leg.state.fl.us/statuTes/index.cfm?App_mode=Display_Statute&Search_String=&URL=Ch0960/Sec001.HTM

Gansz v. State, 888 P.2d 256, Colo., January 17, 1995.

Goff v. State, 387 Md. 327, 875 A.2d 132, June 6, 2005.

Hoile v. State, 404 Md. 591, 948 A.2d 30, May 7, 2008.

Idaho Misdemeanor Criminal Rule 2.1, Social Security Numbers. As of September 11, 2009:
http://www.isc.idaho.gov/rules/misd2-1.txt

Idaho Statutes, Title 9, Evidence, Chapter 3, Public Writings, Section 340C, Records Exempt from Disclosure: Personnel Records, Personal Information, Health Records, Professional Discipline. As of September 11, 2009:
http://www3.state.id.us/cgi-bin/newidst?sctid=090030040C.K

———, Title 18, Crimes and Punishments, Chapter 86, Human Trafficking, Section 8604, Restitution: Rehabilitation. As of September 11, 2009:
http://www.legislature.idaho.gov/idstat/Title18/T18CH86SECT18-8604.htm

———, Title 19, Criminal Procedure, Chapter 53, Compensation of Victims of Crimes, Section 5304, Restitution for Crime Victims: Orders to Be Separate, When Restitution Is Not Appropriate, Other Remedies, Evidentiary Hearings, Definitions. As of September 11, 2009:
http://www.legislature.idaho.gov/idstat/Title19/T19CH53SECT19-5304.htm

———, Title 19, Criminal Procedure, Chapter 57, Address Confidentiality for Victims of Violence. As of September 11, 2009:
http://www.legislature.idaho.gov/idstat/Title19/T19CH57.htm

———, Title 39, Health and Safety, Chapter 63, Domestic Violence Crime Prevention, Section 6316, Law Enforcement Officers: Training, Powers, Duties. As of September 14, 2009:
http://www.legislature.idaho.gov/idstat/Title39/T39CH63SECT39-6316.htm

———, Title 72, Worker's Compensation and Related Laws: Industrial Commission, Chapter 10, Crime Victims Compensation, Section 1003, Definitions. As of September 11, 2009:
http://www.legislature.idaho.gov/idstat/Title72/T72CH10SECT72-1003.htm

———, Title 72, Worker's Compensation and Related Laws: Industrial Commission, Chapter 10, Crime Victims Compensation, Section 1019, Compensation Benefits. As of September 11, 2009:
http://www.legislature.idaho.gov/idstat/Title72/T72CH10SECT72-1019.htm

In re Andrew C., 215 Ariz. 366, 160 P.3d 687, Ariz. Ct. App., June 21, 2007.

In re K.P., 311 N.J. Super. 123, 709 A.2d 315, December 29, 1997.

In re Michael H., 360 S.C. 540, 602 S.E.2d 729, July 23, 2002, heard; August 30, 2004, refiled.

In re Michelle G., 217 Ariz. 340, 173 P.3d 1041, Ariz. Ct. App., January 10, 2008.

In re Richard B., 216 Ariz. 127, 163 P.3d 1077, Ariz. Ct. App., August 7, 2007.

In re Stephanie B., 204 Ariz. 466, 65 P.3d 114, Ariz. Ct. App., March 27, 2003.

In re Terrence M., 368 S.C. 276, 628 S.E.2d 295, S.C. Ct. App., March 16, 2006.

In re William L., 211 Ariz. 236, 119 P.3d 1039, Ariz. Ct. App., September 15, 2005.

Indiana Code, Title 35, Criminal Law and Procedure, Article 40, Victim Rights, Chapter 2, Applicability, Standing to Invoke Rights.

Juliano v. State, 166 Md. App. 531, 890 A.2d 847, Md. Ct. Spec. App., January 27, 2006.

Kenna v. United States Dist. Court, 435 F.3d 1011, 9th Cir., January 20, 2006.

Kenna v. United States Dist. Court, 453 F.3d 1136, 9th Cir., July 5, 2006.

Kilpatrick, Dean G., David Beatty, and Susan Smith Howley, *The Rights of Crime Victims: Does Legal Protection Make a Difference?* Washington, D.C.: U.S. Department of Justice, Office of Justice Programs, National Institute of Justice, 1998. As of September 11, 2009:
http://purl.access.gpo.gov/GPO/LPS91303

Kilpatrick, Dean G., C. L. Best, and S. A. Falsetti, *South Carolina Speaks Out: Attitudes About Crime and Victims' Rights*, Charleston, S.C.: Medical University of South Carolina Press, 1993.

Kilpatrick, Dean G., and Ritchie Tidwell, *Victims Rights and Services in South Carolina: The Dream, the Law, the Reality—Final Report*, Charleston, S.C.: Crime Victims Research and Treatment Center, Department of Psychiatry and Behavioral Sciences, Medical University of South Carolina, 1989.

Klein, Stephen P., Richard A. Berk, and Laura J. Hickman, *Race and the Decision to Seek the Death Penalty in Federal Cases*, Santa Monica, Calif.: RAND Corporation, TR-389-NIJ, 2006. As of October 21, 2009:
http://www.rand.org/pubs/technical_reports/TR389/

Lamb v. Kontgias, 169 Md. App. 466, 901 A.2d 860, July 3, 2006; *cert. denied*, 395 Md. 57, 909 A.2d 259, October 18, 2006; *cert. denied*, 169 Md. App. 466, 901 A.2d 260, July 3, 2006; *cert. denied*, 127 S. Ct. 1875, 549 U.S. 1304, March 26, 2007.

Lancaster v. State, 180 Md. App. 1, 948 A.2d 102, May 9, 2008.

Lawson v. State, 389 Md. 570, 886 A.2d 876, Md. Ct. App., November 28, 2005.

Lincoln v. Holt, 215 Ariz. 21, 156 P.3d 438, Ariz. Ct. App., April 26, 2007.

Lopez-Sanchez v. State, 155 Md. App. 680, 843 A.2d 915, March 8, 2004; affirmed, 388 Md. 214, 879 A.2d 695, Md. Ct. App., July 28, 2005.

Lynn v. Reinstein, 205 Ariz. 186, 68 P.3d 412, May 19, 2003.

Marbury v. Madison, 5 U.S. 137, February 24, 1803.

Maryland Code, Commercial Law, Title 17, Disposition of Abandoned Property, Subtitle 3, Abandoned Property in This State, Section 317, Disposition of Funds Received Under Title.

———, Correctional Services, Title 7, Parole, Release on Mandatory Supervision, and Executive Clemency, Subtitle 3, Eligibility for Parole, Parole Hearings, Section 309, Medical Parole.

———, Correctional Services, Title 8, State and Local Correctional System: Generally, Subtitle 1, Standards for Correctional Facilities, Section 103, Establishment of Standards.

———, Criminal Law, Title 9, Crimes Against Public Administration, Subtitle 3, Obstructing Justice, Section 302, Inducing False Testimony or Avoidance of Subpoena.

———, Criminal Law, Title 9, Crimes Against Public Administration, Subtitle 3, Obstructing Justice, Section 303, Retaliation for Testimony.

———, Criminal Procedure, Title 3, Incompetency and Criminal Responsibility in Criminal Cases, Section 123, Notification of Victim.

———, Criminal Procedure, Title 11, Victims and Witnesses, Subtitle 1, General Provisions, Part I, Definitions, Rights Available Throughout Proceedings, Section 103, Leave to Appeal.

———, Criminal Procedure, Title 11, Victims and Witnesses, Subtitle 6, Restitution and Other Payments, Section 601, Defined Terms.

———, Criminal Procedure, Title 11, Victims and Witnesses, Subtitle 6, Restitution and Other Payments, Section 603, Restitution Determination.

———, Criminal Procedure, Title 11, Victims and Witnesses, Subtitle 6, Restitution and Other Payments, Section 606, Payment of Restitution.

———, Criminal Procedure, Title 11, Victims and Witnesses, Subtitle 6, Restitution and Other Payments, Section 608, Recording and Indexing of Judgment.

———, Criminal Procedure, Title 11, Victims and Witnesses, Subtitle 6, Restitution and Other Payments, Section 610, Judgment of District Court.

———, Criminal Procedure, Title 11, Victims and Witnesses, Subtitle 6, Restitution and Other Payments, Section 613, Stay of Execution of Sentence.

———, Criminal Procedure, Title 11, Victims and Witnesses, Subtitle 6, Restitution and Other Payments, Section 619, Scope of Authority of Court.

———, Criminal Procedure, Title 11, Victims and Witnesses, Subtitle 8, Criminal Injuries Compensation Board, Section 808, Eligibility for Awards.

———, Criminal Procedure, Title 11, Victims and Witnesses, Subtitle 8, Criminal Injuries Compensation Board, Section 809, Filing of Claims.

———, Criminal Procedure, Title 11, Victims and Witnesses, Subtitle 8, Criminal Injuries Compensation Board, Section 813, Emergency Award Pending Final Decision.

———, Criminal Procedure, Title 11, Victims and Witnesses, Subtitle 9, Victims and Witnesses: Services, Section 919, Grant Program.

———, Family Law, Title 4, Spouses, Subtitle 5, Domestic Violence, Part IV, Address Confidentiality Program.

Maryland Rules, Title I, General Provisions, Chapter 300, General Provisions, Rule 326, Proceedings Regarding Victims and Victims' Representatives.

———, Title 5, Evidence, Chapter 600, Evidence, Rule 615, Exclusion of Witnesses.

———, Title 8, Appellate Review in the Court of Appeals and Court of Special Appeals, Chapter 100, General Provisions, Rule 111, Designation of Parties, References.

———, Title 8, Appellate Review in the Court of Appeals and Court of Special Appeals, Chapter 200, Obtaining Review in Court of Special Appeals, Rule 204, Application for Leave to Appeal to Court of Special Appeals.

———, Title 15, Other Special Proceedings, Chapter 200, Contempt, Rule 206, Constructive Civil Contempt.

———, Title 16, Courts, Judges, and Attorneys, Chapter 1000, Access to Court Records, Rule 1008, Electronic Records and Retrieval.

———, Title 16, Courts, Judges, and Attorneys, Chapter 1000, Access to Court Records, Rule 1009, Court Order Denying or Permitting Inspection of Case Record.

Maryland v. Snowden, 385 Md. 64, 867 A.2d 314, Md. Ct. App., February 7, 2005.

Merritt, Nancy, Terry Fain, and Susan Turner, *Oregon's Measure 11 Sentencing Reform: Implementation and System Impact*, Santa Monica, Calif.: RAND Corporation, TR-142-NIJ, 2004. As of October 21, 2009: http://www.rand.org/pubs/technical_reports/TR142/

Nasci v. Pope, No. 29,878, N.M., November 8, 2006.

National Center for State Courts, and American Prosecutors Research Institute, *A Workload Assessment Study for the New Mexico Trial Court Judiciary, New Mexico District Attorneys' Offices and New Mexico Public Defender Department: Final Report*, June 2007. As of September 11, 2009: http://nmsc.isrunm.net/nmsc_reports/workload/

National Crime Victim Law Institute, "History of NCVLI," Web page, undated (a). As of September 15, 2009: http://www.ncvli.org/history.html

———, "NAVRA: The National Alliance of Victims' Rights Attorneys," Web page, undated (b). As of September 15, 2009: http://www.ncvli.org/navra.html

NCSC and APRI—*see* National Center for State Courts and American Prosecutor Research Institute.

NCVLI—*see* National Crime Victim Law Institute.

New Jersey Administrative Code, Title 10A, Corrections, Chapter 9, Classification Process, Subchapter 10, Residential Community Program Notification Committee, Section 1, Responsibilities of the Residential Community Program Notification Committee.

———, Title 10A, Corrections, Chapter 9, Classification Process, Subchapter 10, Residential Community Program Notification Committee, Section 3, Residential Community Program Notification Committee Decision Making Criteria for Placement in a Residential Community Program.

———, Title 10A, Corrections, Chapter 22, Records, Subchapter 2, Government Records, Section 11, Juvenile Records and Information.

———, Title 10A, Corrections, Chapter 31, Adult County Correctional Facilities, Subchapter 6, Management Information System and Records, Section 5, Information Pertaining to a Victim(s).

———, Title 10A, Corrections, Chapter 71, Parole, Subchapter 6, Supervision, Section 12, Parole Supervision for Life.

———, Title 13, Law and Public Safety, Chapter 18, Executive and Administrative Service, Subchapter 11, Organization of the Motor Vehicle Commission, Section 3, Government Records, Examination, Purchase of Copies, Exemption.

New Jersey Permanent Statutes, Title 2A, Administration of Civil and Criminal Justice, Section 53A-21, Civil Cause of Action for Bias Crime Victims.

———, Title 2C, The New Jersey Code of Criminal Justice, Section 14-12, Conditions Placed upon Release of Certain Defendants.

———, Title 2C, The New Jersey Code of Criminal Justice, Section 17-3, Criminal Mischief.

———, Title 2C, The New Jersey Code of Criminal Justice, Section 21-17.4, Action by Person Defrauded by Unauthorized Use of Personal Identifying Information.

———, Title 2C, The New Jersey Code of Criminal Justice, Section 44-8, Convicted Defendants, Prior Restrictions Continued.

———, Title 2C, The New Jersey Code of Criminal Justice, Section 45-1, Conditions of Suspension or Probation.

———, Title 2C, The New Jersey Code of Criminal Justice, Section 45-2, Period of Suspension or Probation, Modification of Conditions, Discharge of Defendant.

———, Title 5, Amusements, Public Exhibitions and Meetings, Section 9-13.17, Offset of Certain Lottery Prizes Required for Payment of Certain Debts to State Agencies.

———, Title 52, State Government, Departments and Officers, Section 4B-3.2, Victims of Crime Compensation Agency, Executive Director, Review Board.

———, Title 52, State Government, Departments and Officers, Section 4B-8, Attorney Fees and Costs.

———, Title 52, State Government, Departments and Officers, Section 4B-11, Victim Compensation.

———, Title 52, State Government, Departments and Officers, Section 4B-25, Victim Counseling Service.

———, Title 52, State Government, Departments and Officers, Section 4B-42, Victim-Witness Rights Information Program.

———, Title 52, State Government, Departments and Officers, Section 4B-44, Standards for Law Enforcement Agencies to Ensure Rights of Crime Victims.

New Mexico Code, Chapter 28, Human Rights, Article 11, Assistance Animal, Section 5, Findings and Purpose, Interference with Qualified Assistance Animals Prohibited, Criminal and Civil Penalties.

———, Chapter 30, Criminal Offenses, Article 1, General Provisions, Section 15, Alleged Victims of Domestic Abuse, Stalking or Sexual Assault, Forbearance of Costs.

———, Chapter 30, Criminal Offenses, Article 9, Sexual Offenses, Section 21.

———, Chapter 30, Criminal Offenses, Article 16, Larceny, Section 24.1, Theft of Identity, Obtaining Identity by Electronic Fraud.

———, Chapter 31, Criminal Procedure, Article 17, Victim Restitution, Section 1, Victim Restitution.

———, Chapter 31, Criminal Procedure, Article 25, Victim Counselor Confidentiality, Sections 1–6, Victim Counselor Confidentiality Act.

———, Chapter 31, Criminal Procedure, Article 26, Victims of Crime, Section 9, Procedures for Providing Victims with Notice of Rights and Information Regarding Prosecution of a Criminal Offense, District Attorneys.

———, Chapter 31, Criminal Procedure, Article 26, Victims of Crime, Section 10.1, Crime Victim Presence at Court Proceedings, Plea Agreement Notification.

———, Chapter 40, Domestic Affairs, Article 13, Family Violence Protection, Section 3.3.

———, Chapter 40, Domestic Affairs, Article 13, Family Violence Protection, Section 11, Substitute Address.

———, Chapter 40, Domestic Affairs, Article 13, Family Violence Protection, Section 6, Service of Order, Duration, Penalty, Remedies Not Exclusive.

New Mexico Constitution, Article II, Bill of Rights, Section 24, Victim's Rights.

New Mexico Rules of Criminal Procedure for the Magistrate Courts, Article 4, Release Provisions, Rule 6-401, Bail.

New Mexico Rules of Evidence, Article 11, Witnesses, Rule 611, Mode and Order of Interrogation and Presentation.

New Mexico Rules of Procedure for the Municipal Courts, Article 4, Release Provisions, Rule 8-401, Bail.

New York Laws, Executive, Fair Treatment Standards for Crime Victims, Section 649, Miscellaneous.

North Carolina General Statutes, Title 15A, Criminal Procedure Act, Section 840, No Ground for Relief.

North Dakota Century Code, Title 12.1, Criminal Code, Chapter 34, Fair Treatment of Victims and Witnesses, Section 5, Cause of Action for Damages or Injunctive Relief.

Opert v. Criminal Injuries Comp. Bd., 403 Md. 587, 943 A.2d 1229, Md. Ct. App., March 11, 2008.

Patterson v. Mahoney, 210 Ariz. 453, 199 P.3d 708, Ariz. Ct. App., December 18, 2008.

P.M. v. Gould, 212 Ariz. 541, 136 P.3d 223, Ariz. Ct. App., May 23, 2006.

President's Task Force on Victims of Crime, *Final Report*, Washington, D.C., December 1982. As of September 11, 2009:
http://www.ojp.usdoj.gov/ovc/publications/presdntstskforcrprt/welcome.html

Public Law 97-291, Victim and Witness Protection Act, October 12, 1982.

Public Law 98-473, Victims of Crime Act, October 12, 1984.

Public Law 101-647, Victims' Rights and Restitution Act, March 20, 1990.

Public Law 103-322, Violent Crime Control and Law Enforcement Act, September 13, 1994.

Public Law 104-132, Antiterrorism and Effective Death Penalty Act, April 24, 1996.

Public Law 105-6, Victim Rights Clarification Act, March 19, 1997.

Public Law 108-405, Justice for All Act, October 30, 2004.

Public Law 108-405, Title I, Crime Victims' Rights Act, October 30, 2004.

Reif v. Kaster, 363 B.R. 107, Bankr.D.Ariz., February 12, 2007.

Riley, K. Jack, Nancy Rodriguez, Greg Ridgeway, Dionne Barnes-Proby, Terry Fain, Nell Griffith Forge, Vincent Webb, and Linda J. Demaine, *Just Cause or Just Because? Prosecution and Plea-Bargaining Resulting in Prison Sentences on Low-Level Drug Charges in California and Arizona*, Santa Monica, Calif.: RAND Corporation, MG-288-RWJ, 2005. As of October 21, 2009: http://www.rand.org/pubs/monographs/MG288/

Roberts v. State, 130 P.3d 1005, Colo., February 13, 2006.

Robey v. State, 397 Md. 449, 918 A.2d 499, March 14, 2007.

Smith, Barbara E., and Susan Hillenbrand, "Making Victims Whole Again: Restitution, Victim-Offender Reconciliation Programs, and Compensation," in Robert C. Davis, Arthur Lurigio, and Wesley Skogan, eds., *Victims of Crime*, 2nd ed., Thousand Oaks, Calif.: Sage Publications, 1999, pp. 247–249.

South Carolina Attorney General Opinion No. 07-034.

South Carolina Code of Laws, Title 16, Crimes and Offenses, Chapter 1, Felonies and Misdemeanors, Accessories, Section 130, Persons Not Eligible for Diversion Program.

———, Title 16, Crimes and Offenses, Chapter 3, Offenses Against the Person, Article 13, Compensation of Victims of Crime, Section 1180, Amount of Award, Apportionment Among Multiple Claimants, Rejection of Application for Award.

———, Title 16, Crimes and Offenses, Chapter 3, Offenses Against the Person, Article 13, Compensation of Victims of Crime, Section 1230, Claim Filed on Behalf of Minor or Incompetent, Time Limitations.

———, Title 16, Crimes and Offenses, Chapter 3, Offenses Against the Person, Article 15, Victim and Witness Service, Section 1525, Arrest or Detention of Person Accused of Committing Offense, Notification to Victims, Protection of Witnesses, Notification of Bond Proceedings, Juvenile Detention Hearing.

———, Title 16, Crimes and Offenses, Chapter 3, Offenses Against the Person, Article 15, Victim and Witness Service, Section 1530, Notification of Victim of Release, Escape or Transfer of Accused.

———, Title 16, Crimes and Offenses, Chapter 3, Offenses Against the Person, Article 15, Victim and Witness Service, Section 1535, Summary Court's Duty to Notify Victim of Victim's Rights, Form for Victim Impact Statement.

———, Title 16, Crimes and Offenses, Chapter 3, Offenses Against the Person, Article 15, Victim and Witness Service, Section 1555, Expert Witness Fees, Distribution, Maintenance and Use of Victim's Impact Statements.

———, Title 16, Crimes and Offenses, Chapter 3, Offenses Against the Person, Article 17, Harassment and Stalking, Section 1735, Law Enforcement Officer Empowered to Sign Warrant in Place of Victim.

———, Title 16, Crimes and Offenses, Chapter 3, Offenses Against the Person, Article 17, Harassment and Stalking, Section 1740, Mental Health Evaluations of Persons Convicted of Stalking or Harassment, Notice to Victim in Person of Unsupervised Release.

———, Title 16, Crimes and Offenses, Chapter 3, Offenses Against the Person, Article 17, Harassment and Stalking, Section 1770, Form and Content of Temporary Restraining Order.

———, Title 16, Crimes and Offenses, Chapter 8, Offenses Promoting Civil Disorder, Section 250, Preventing Witness or Victim from Testifying, Penalty, Coerced Person's Right to Bring Civil Action.

———, Title 17, Criminal Procedures, Chapter 28, Access to Justice Post-Conviction DNA Testing, Article 1, Post-Conviction DNA Procedures, Section 50, Application for Testing, Notification of Prosecutor, Custodian of Evidence, and Victim, Dismissal, Successive Applications.

———, Title 17, Criminal Procedures, Chapter 28, Access to Justice Post-Conviction DNA Testing, Article 1, Post-Conviction DNA Procedures, Section 90, Hearing, Factors to Be Proved, Orders Relating to DNA Samples.

———, Title 17, Criminal Procedures, Chapter 28, Access to Justice Post-Conviction DNA Testing, Article 1, Post-Conviction DNA Procedures, Section 100, Disclosure and Use of Test Results, Motion for New Trial.

———, Title 17, Criminal Procedures, Chapter 28, Access to Justice Post-Conviction DNA Testing, Article 3, Preservation of Evidence, Section 340, Petition for Destruction of Evidence Prior to Expiration of Required Time Period.

———, Title 24, Corrections, Jails, Probations, Paroles and Pardons, Chapter 1, Department of Corrections, Section 295, Employment of Inmates for Work Involving Exportation of Products, Deductions from Wages.

———, Title 24, Corrections, Jails, Probations, Paroles and Pardons, Chapter 21, Probation, Parole and Pardon, Article 1, Board of Probation, Parole, and Pardon Services, Section 30, Meetings, Parole and Pardon Panels.

———, Title 24, Corrections, Jails, Probations, Paroles and Pardons, Chapter 21, Probation, Parole and Pardon, Article 1, Board of Probation, Parole, and Pardon Services, Section 35, Administrative Recommendations Available to Victim Prior to Parole Hearing.

———, Title 24, Corrections, Jails, Probations, Paroles and Pardons, Chapter 21, Probation, Parole and Pardon, Article 7, Parole, Release for Good Conduct, Section 710, Film, Videotape, or Other Electronic Information May Be Considered by Board in Parole Determination.

———, Title 40, Professions and Occupations, Chapter 47, Physicians, Surgeons and Osteopaths, Article 1, General Provisions, Section 190, Disclosure of Information Relating to Proceedings, Public Access, Information Relating to Patients and Witnesses.

———, Title 44, Health, Chapter 24, Commitment of Children in Need of Mental Health Treatment, Section 150, Psychiatric Evaluations of Children, Notification of Victims.

South Carolina Constitution, Article I, Declaration of Rights, Section 24, Victims' Bill of Rights.

Stachowski v. State, 403 Md. 1, 939 A.2d 158, Md. Ct. App., January 9, 2008.

State v. Aker, 137 N.M. 561, 113 P.3d 384, N.M. Ct. App., April 12, 2005.

State v. Armstrong, 218 Ariz. 451, 189 P.3d 378, July 29, 2008.

State v. Barlow, 372 S.C. 534, 643 S.E.2d 682, March 26, 2007.

State v. Billsie, 2006 UT 13, 131 P.3d 239, February 28, 2006.

State ex rel. Brandenburg v. Blackmer, 137 N.M. 258, 110 P.3d 66, April 7, 2005.

State v. Bocharski, 218 Ariz. 476, 189 P.3d 403, August 8, 2008.

State v. Cabrera, 2007 UT App 194, 163 P.3d 707, June 7, 2007.

State v. Card, 146 Idaho 111, 190 P.3d 930, Idaho Ct. App., July 2, 2008.

State v. Carreon, 210 Ariz. 54, 107 P.3d 900, February 24, 2005.

State v. Casey, 2002 UT 29, 44 P.3d 756, March 12, 2002.

State v. Cheeney, 144 Idaho 294, 160 P.3d 451, Idaho Ct. App., May 29, 2007.

State v. Collins, 142 N.M. 419, 166 P.3d 480, N.M. Ct. App., June 19, 2007.

State ex rel. Romley v. Dairman, 208 Ariz. 484, 95 P.3d 548, Ariz. Ct. App., August 10, 2004.

State v. Deisz, 145 Idaho 826, 186 P.3d 682, Idaho Ct. App., May 27, 2008.

State v. Disher, 2008 Colo. LEXIS 432, Colo., April 21, 2008.

State v. Dixon, 216 Ariz. 18, 162 P.3d 657, July 11, 2007.

State v. Doe, 140 Idaho 873, 103 P.3d 967, Idaho Ct. App., December 20, 2004.

State v. Doe, 146 Idaho 277, 192 P.3d 1101, Idaho Ct. App., June 9, 2008.

State v. Ellison, 213 Ariz. 116, 140 P.3d 899, August 9, 2006.

State ex rel. Thomas v. Foreman, 211 Ariz. 153, 118 P.3d 1117, Ariz. Ct. App., September 1, 2005.

State v. Garcia, 137 N.M. 583, 113 P.3d 406, N.M. Ct. App., April 28, 2005.

State v. Garnett, 384 Md. 466, 863 A.2d 1007, Md. Ct. App., December 22, 2004.

State v. Garnett, 172 Md. App. 558, 916 A.2d 393, Md. Ct. Spec. App., February 2, 2007; *cert. denied* 399 Md. 594, 925 A.2d 633, Md. Ct. App., June 8, 2007.

State v. Garza, 216 Ariz. 56, 163 P.3d 1006, June 29, 2007; cert. denied 128 S. Ct. 890, January 7, 2008.

State v. Gilchrist, 381 N.J. Super. 138, 885 A.2d 29, November 3, 2005.

State v. Glassel, 211 Ariz. 33, 116 P.3d 1193, August 10, 2005.

State v. Gonzales, 144 Idaho 775, 171 P.3d 266, Idaho Ct. App., August 7, 2007.

State v. Guadagni, 218 Ariz. 1, 178 P.3d 473, Ariz. Ct. App., February 29, 2008.

State v. Hampton, 213 Ariz. 156, 140 P.3d 950, August 15, 2006; cert. denied, 127 S. Ct. 972, January 8, 2007.

State ex rel. Hance v. Arizona Bd. of Pardons and Paroles, 178 Ariz. 591, 875 P.2d 824, Ariz. Ct. App., October 26, 1993.

State v. Herrera, 135 N.M. 79, 84 P.3d 696, N.M. Ct. App., December 4, 2003.

State v. Hight, 2008 UT App 118, 182 P.3d 922, April 3, 2008.

State v. Houey, 375 S.C. 106, 651 S.E.2d 314, September 10, 2007.

State v. Jones, 141 Idaho 673, 115 P.3d 764, Idaho Ct. App., May 27, 2005.

State ex rel. Thomas v. Klein, 214 Ariz. 205, 150 P.3d 778, Ariz. Ct. App., January 11, 2007.

State v. Korsen, 141 Idaho 445, 111 P.3d 130, April 1, 2005.

State v. Lamar, 205 Ariz. 431, 72 P.3d 831, July 17, 2003.

State v. Lampien, 2008 Ida. App. LEXIS 138, Idaho Ct. App., November 3, 2008.

State v. Lane, Nos. 20070878, 20061126, S.C. Utah, oral argument September 3, 2008.

State v. Lane, 2009 UT 35, 212 P.3d 529, June 12, 2009.

State v. Leon, 142 Idaho 705, 132 P.3d 462, Idaho Ct. App., January 10, 2006.

State v. Leonard, 167 P.3d 178, Colo. Ct. App., September 27, 2007.

State v. Lutes, 141 Idaho 911, 120 P.3d 299, Idaho Ct. App., June 10, 2005.

State v. Madrid, 207 Ariz. 296, 85 P.3d 1054, Ariz. Ct. App., March 18, 2004.

State v. Martinez, 218 Ariz. 421, 189 P.3d 348, July 25, 2008.

State v. Martinez, 166 P.3d 223, Colo. Ct. App., May 17, 2007.

State v. Martinez, 143 N.M. 428, 176 P.3d 1160, N.M. Ct. App., February 5, 2008.

State v. Means, 191 N.J. 610, 926 A.2d 328, July 11, 2007.

State v. Mercer, 143 Idaho 108, 138 P.3d 308, March 20, 2006.

State v. Mosley, 167 P.3d 157, Colo. Ct. App., September 27, 2007.

State v. Muhammad, 145 N.J. 23, 678 A.2d 164, June 28, 1996.

State v. Payne, 146 Idaho 548, 199 P.3d 123, December 15, 2008.

State v. Reyes, 166 P.3d 301, Colo. Ct. App., June 28, 2007.

State v. Roque, 213 Ariz. 193, 141 P.3d 368, August 14, 2006.

State v. Schultz, 2008 Ida. App. LEXIS 149, Idaho Ct. App., December 15, 2008.

State v. Shafer, 144 Idaho 370, 161 P.3d 689, Idaho Ct. App., March 8, 2007.

State v. Smith, 181 P.3d 324, Colo. Ct. App., August 23, 2007.

State v. Smith, 144 Idaho 687, 169 P.3d 275, Idaho Ct. App., August 1, 2007.

State v. Thompson, 181 P.3d 1143, Colo., April 7, 2008.

State v. Towery, 204 Ariz. 386, 64 P.3d 828, February 26, 2003.

State v. Tucker, 215 Ariz. 298, 160 P.3d 177, May 13, 2007.

State v. Wakefield, 190 N.J. 397, 921 A.2d 954, May 7, 2007.

State v. Williams, 404 N.J. Super. 147, 960 A.2d 805, December 12, 2008.

State v. Worthen, 2008 UT App 23, 177 P.3d 664, January 25, 2008.

Surland v. State, 392 Md. 17, 895 A.2d 1034, Md. Ct. App., April 11, 2006.

Texas Constitution, Article I, Bill of Rights, Section 30, Rights of Crime Victims. As of September 11, 2009:
http://www.statutes.legis.state.tx.us/SOTWDocs/CN/htm/CN.1.htm

Torrence v S.C. Dept. of Corr., 373 S.C. 586, 646 S.E.2d 866, May 7, 2007.

Town of Gilbert Prosecutor's Office v. Downie, 218 Ariz. 466, 189 P.3d 393, August 4, 2008.

Tushnet, Mark V., *The NAACP's Legal Strategy Against Segregated Education, 1925–1950*, Chapel Hill, N.C.: University of North Carolina Press, 2004.

United States v. Lay, 456 F. Supp. 2d 869, S.D. Tex., October 17, 2006; *mand. denied*, 06-20848, 5th Cir., 2006.

U.S. Code, Title 18, Crimes and Criminal Procedure.

———, Title 18, Crimes and Criminal Procedure, Chapter 237, Crime Victims' Rights.

———, Title 42, Public Health and Welfare.

U.S. Department of Justice, Office of Justice Programs, *Four Years Later: A Report on the President's Task Force on Victims of Crime*, Washington, D.C., May 1986. As of September 11, 2009:
http://www.ncjrs.gov/pdffiles1/ovc/102834.pdf

Utah Administrative Code, Pardons (Board of), Title R671, Administration, Chapter 203, Victim Input and Notification, Section 1, General Provisions.

———, Pardons (Board of), Title R671, Administration, Chapter 203, Victim Input and Notification, Section 2, Notification.

———, Pardons (Board of), Title R671, Administration, Chapter 203, Victim Input and Notification, Section 3, Right to Attend, Right to Testify.

———, Pardons (Board of), Title R671, Administration, Chapter 203, Victim Input and Notification, Section 4, Victim Statements and Testimony.

———, Pardons (Board of), Title R671, Administration, Chapter 203, Victim Input and Notification, Section 5, Victim Impact Hearings.

———, Pardons (Board of), Title R671, Administration, Chapter 315, Pardons, Section 1, Pardons.

———, Pardons (Board of), Title R671, Administration, Chapter 403, Restitution, Section 1, Policy.

Utah Code, Title 63M, Governor's Programs, Chapter 7, Criminal Justice and Substance Abuse, Part 5, Crime Victims Reparations Act.

———, Title 76, Utah Criminal Code, Chapter 3, Punishments, Part 4, Limitations and Special Provisions on Sentences, Section 402, Conviction of Lower Degree of Offense: Procedure and Limitations.

———, Title 77, Utah Code of Criminal Procedure, Chapter 37, Victims' Rights, Section 4, Additional Rights: Children.

———, Title 77, Utah Code of Criminal Procedure, Chapter 38, Rights of Crime Victims Act, Section 11, Enforcement, Appellate Review, No Right to Money Damages.

———, Title 77, Utah Code of Criminal Procedure, Chapter 38A, Crime Victims Restitution Act, Part 3, Restitution Requirements, Section 302, Restitution Criteria.

———, Title 77, Utah Code of Criminal Procedure, Chapter 38A, Crime Victims Restitution Act, Part 4, Restitution Judgments.

———, Title 78A, Judiciary and Judicial Administration, Chapter 6, Juvenile Court Act of 1996, Part 1, General Provisions, Section 114, Hearings, Public Excluded, Exceptions, Victims Admitted, Minor's Cases Heard Separately from Adult Cases, Minor or Parents or Custodian Heard Separately, Continuance of Hearing, Consolidation of Proceedings Involving More Than One Minor.

———, Title 78A, Judiciary and Judicial Administration, Chapter 6, Juvenile Court Act of 1996, Part 1, General Provisions, Section 121, Entry of Judgement [sic] for Fine or Restitution, Transfer for Collection.

———, Title 78A, Judiciary and Judicial Administration, Chapter 6, Juvenile Court Act of 1996, Part 11, Miscellaneous Provisions, Section 1105, Expungement of Juvenile Court Record: Petition, Procedure.

———, Title 78B, Judicial Code, Chapter 3, Actions and Venue, Part 1, Actions: Right to Sue and Be Sued, Section 110, Defense to Civil Action for Damages Resulting from Commission of Crime.

Utah Rules of Criminal Procedure, Rule 14, Subpoenas.

———, Rule 15.5, Out of Court Statement and Testimony of Child Victims or Child Witnesses of Sexual or Physical Abuse: Conditions of Admissibility.

Utah Rules of Judicial Administration, Part I, Judicial Council Rules of Judicial Administration, Chapter 4, Operation of the Courts, Article 2, Court Records, Exhibits and Files, Section 202, Purpose.

Williams v. State, 385 Md. 50, 867 A.2d 305, Md. Ct. App., 2005.